Techniques of Drawing and Painting

WILDLIFE

Techniques of Drawing and Painting

WILDLIFE

Fredric Sweney

REINHOLD PUBLISHING CORPORATION · NEW YORK

© 1959

Reinhold Publishing Corporation

Printed in the United States of America

Designed by Myron Hall 3rd and Fredric Sweney

Type set by Philmac Typographers

Printed by Miller-Johnson, Inc.

Bound by Russell-Rutter

Color plates by Bijutsa Shuppan Sha, Japan

Library of Congress Catalogue Card No. 59-11974

To my wife Ruth, and my son Bill,

and to my friends whose patience,

encouragement, and guidance

helped make this book possible.

SWENEY

CONTENTS

FOREWORD

Until the light from the lamp of a Spanish explorer illuminated the walls of a cave at Altamira in Northern Spain, man's earliest art efforts had been hidden from the world for over fifteen thousand years. The flood of light, pushing back the darkness of the cave, revealed that the first art impression of the hunter-artist was the beauty found in the animal world.

Using only a piece of flint as a carving tool, with red and yellow ochres and black to define and stain the incised areas, he left his drawings and paintings for Time to discover.

The ability of the early hunter-artist is all the more remarkable when one considers the trying conditions that faced him. He had practically no materials; his only light was a small flickering flame in his subterranean studio. Furthermore, he was forced to rely on memory for details and movements of his subject matter — the animals that provided food and clothing for his family and himself.

With the advance of civilization and its inventions, the wildlife artist of today has at his disposal the many books and study aids that our paleolithic artist did not have.

The artist who wants to specialize in wildlife painting will have many problems with which to contend. A natural liking and understanding of animals and birds is foremost in the development of a wildlife artist. The ability to sense or anticipate the reactions of wildlife under various conditions and situations is essential.

All of the fundamentals of drawing should be mastered beforehand. This is a specialized field and is not for the novice. A knowledge of the construction, form, and anatomy of the human figure is necessary for the understanding of animal and bird anatomy.

The purpose of this book is to guide the student of wildlife and nature drawings and to help the professional artist who wants to further his knowledge of bird, fish, and animal painting.

ADDENDA

To concentrate our study of wildlife on a few examples of animals, birds, and fish, rather than try to cover all of the families and species, will simplify the task of understanding the technicalities and the drawing of them.

A wildlife artist should first develop a thorough knowledge of the anatomy of animals, birds, and fish, their habitat and behavior, and then be very discerning in the use of that knowledge. A certain amount of field work will be necessary to achieve this informative background. It is important to the nature artist that subjects be in their correct habitat. For example, a Blackburnian warbler probably would not be seen in a maple woods but more likely be found in a coniferous forest.

In order to study the principles of bird art, the duck family will serve as a criterion for the other members of the class Aves. Most of us are familiar with ducks so we will not be confused by the problem of trying to draw a bird with which we are not too well acquainted.

Once the approach to drawing one species of bird is understood, it will serve as a basis for drawing others. The aerodynamics of a mourning dove are not too far removed from the flight of a mallard duck.

This same theory will be applied to the drawing of fish and animals as well. The brook trout will serve as a model for the fish, and the deer, an animal familiar to most of us, will be the example used for the animals.

There always is that inevitable question of how much anatomy should be in evidence in a painting. Too much anatomy in a drawing is as bad as not enough.

To paint a thin-coated animal, such as a deer, and show every muscle will tend to make it look unnatural and freeze the action. Therefore it is better to *indicate* the flowing muscular action of an animal in a painting.

Needless to say, a library and reference file should be started early since most of the material is of a specialized nature and cannot be assembled hurriedly. The collecting of a file and indexing are explained in the latter portion of this book.

There are available excellent books for the identification of mammals, birds, and fish. Binoculars are almost a necessity for the study of birds and animals. Keeping a bird check list during field trips is interesting and will sharpen the power of observation as well as help in the study of their habitat.

For drawing and taking notes in the field a bound sketch book, a few pencils, a small set of colored pastels, a bottle of fixitive and atomizer complete your materials. A dry medium, such as pastel, is more convenient for taking quick field notes than a wet medium.

FIELD SKETCHES
AND ARTIST'S
SHORTHAND

These action studies were developed from field sketches. A felt pen line, simple washes of lampblack, and white pastel for accent are the mediums.

The study of a white-tail fawn was made with a wash of lampblack, carbon pencil, and three values of white. The whites are a combination of opaque, pencil, and pastel mediums.

13

BIRDS

An understanding and logical approach to bird drawing, their anatomy and aerodynamics, with a progressive demonstration of a bird painting from the original abstract design to the completed work.

SECTION I

"Ibis on Papyrus" from a tomb at Beni Hasan, circa 2000 B.C.

FIELD IDENTIFICATION

An exacting phase of bird art is the identification and coordination of the plumage with the seasons of the year. This is particularly important if the painting is a portrait of a species.

For example, the male mallard duck, which is portrayed quite frequently, passes through two distinct molts or color changes before it reaches its full winter plumage.

The first molt, known as the *eclipse*, begins in early June and usually is completed in August. During this time the mallard drake closely resembles the mallard hen. Its old flight feathers are discarded and replaced with new ones; consequently the bird is grounded and at the mercy of its enemies. The drake generally deserts his mate and family at this time and remains hidden in the reeds until he can fly again.

The second or *pre-nuptial* molt takes place when the drake discards its imitation of the hen's coloring and changes into its winter plumage. For these reasons it is not technically authentic to show the mallard drake in full winter plumage with its mate and ducklings, although they are often portrayed in this manner.

Mallard drake in eclipse molt

Mallard drake in pre-nuptial molt

Full winter plumage of Mallard drake

Ringnecks are occasionally seen with flocks of lesser scaup ducks.

FLIGHT POSITIONS FOR IDENTIFICATION

Not all flight positions are favorable for the identification of a species. Where there are more birds than one in a picture a few should be positioned so that the field marks are easily seen. The three ducks illustrated are of different species but very similar in appearance. Outlawing color as a means of identification in the field, since value and patterns are more dependable, it would be difficult for the novice to identify correctly the ducks illustrated above as the field marks are not too distinct.

The drawing to the right shows the birds in a better flight attitude for identification because the upper-wing field marks are easily seen.

These drawings were executed in transparent lampblack washes and opaque greys.

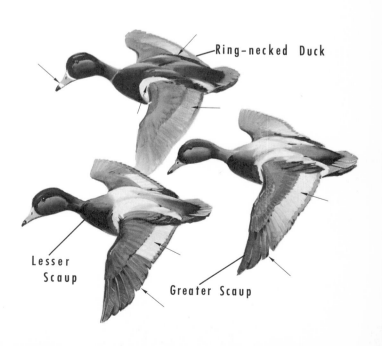

Crown

Ear

Nape

Forehead

Bill

Nail

Nostril

Hind Neck

Side of Neck

Cheek

Chin

Throat

Back

Foreneck

Rump

Chest

Upper Tail Coverts

Tail

Breast

Under Tail Coverts

Flank

Side

Belly

Foot

TOPOGRAPHY OF A BIRD

Whenever possible the use of anatomical and ornithological terms has been avoided. Not before the advanced study of the construction and forms of a bird is a knowledge of ornithological terms necessary.

CROWN — upper section of the head or skull above the line formed by eye and ear opening.

EAR — organ of hearing, located directly in back of the eye and covered by a group of feathers known as the auriculars.

NAPE — upper division of the neck, located directly below the base of the skull; the occipital portion of the skull.

HIND NECK — posterior or rear section of the neck.

SIDE OF NECK — lateral or outer section of the neck.

BACK — upper area of the body, located between the base of the neck and rump; the dorsal region of the spine.

RUMP — lower or pelvic area of the back; the sacrum area.

UPPER-TAIL COVERTS — the grouping of feathers overlaying the base of the tail.

TAIL — posterior extremity of the body.

UNDER-TAIL COVERTS — the feathers located under the base of the tail.

FLANK — posterior area of the sides of the body.

BELLY — abdomen area of the bird.

FOOT — tarsus and toe area between the heel and tip of the toes (see drawings on pages 20 and 32 for heel position and tarsus respectively).

SIDE — area covering the lateral portion of the rib cage; the area between the back and the breast.

BREAST — section between the belly and chest; the breastbone or sternum sections of the rib cage area.

CHEST — area between the lower division of the neck and breast.

FORENECK — anterior or front portion of the neck between the chest and throat area.

THROAT — anterior upper section of the neck.

CHIN — area located on the under section of the skull, at the base of the lower mandible or bill.

CHEEK — side of the head located between the eye and chin.

NOSTRIL — external opening located on the upper area of the mandible or bill.

NAIL — raised section located on the tip of the mandible or bill.

BILL — term employed for the mandible, beak or mouth area.

FOREHEAD — front of the skull.

19

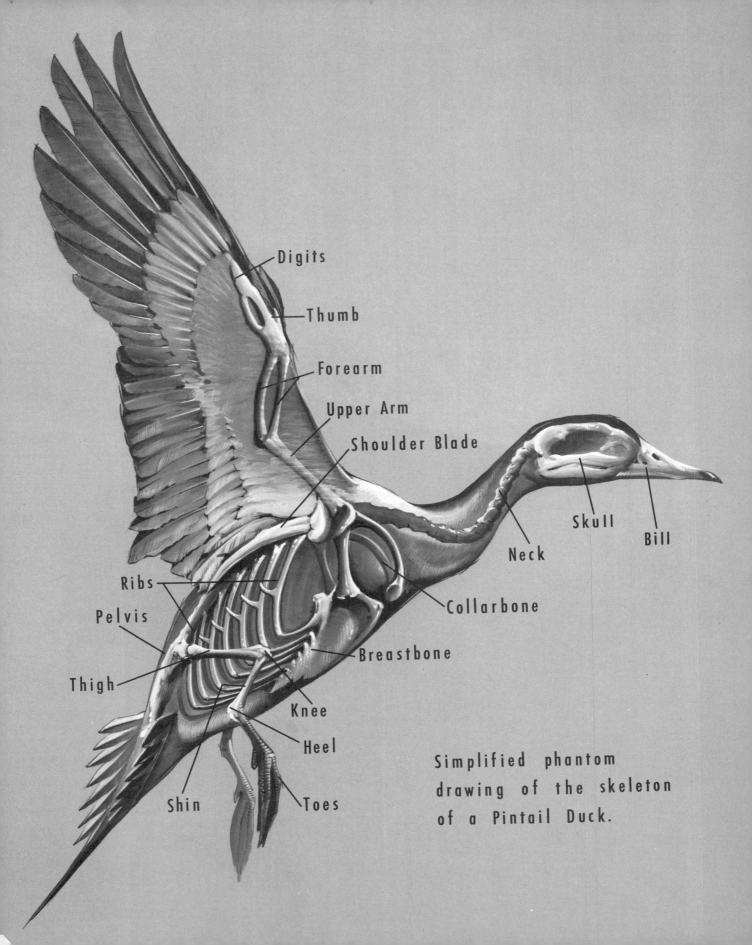

Digits

Thumb

Forearm

Upper Arm

Shoulder Blade

Skull

Bill

Neck

Collarbone

Ribs

Pelvis

Breastbone

Thigh

Knee

Heel

Shin

Toes

Simplified phantom drawing of the skeleton of a Pintail Duck.

THE SKELETON

It is difficult to imagine the millions of years of leisurely evolution necessary to change the awkward flight attempts of the reptile-like bird archaeopteryx into the air-splitting, powered flight of a pintail.

A skeleton closely related to the human form yet structurally different and adaptable for flight is very perplexing. The bone structure of a bird is usually aerated for lightness: the larger the bird the more pneumatic the bone composition; the smaller the bird the more compact.

The phantom drawing of a pintail duck shows the approximate locations of various parts of the skeleton. Basically, bone structures are the same in most birds. The greatest change occurs in the number of vertebrae in the neck and the lengths of the wing bones.

As an example, the construction of a pelican's wing is the same as that of a duck but the bones are longer to conform to its contour.

A knowledge of bone structure is necessary in order to build a solid drawing of a bird, although very little of the skeleton is in evidence in the final painting.

As illustrated, the knee is high in relation to the sides of the body. The section that often is mistakenly called the knee is actually the heel of the bird. The bone extending between the heel and toes compares with the arch of the human foot and is called the tarsus.

21

The use of a bird's tail

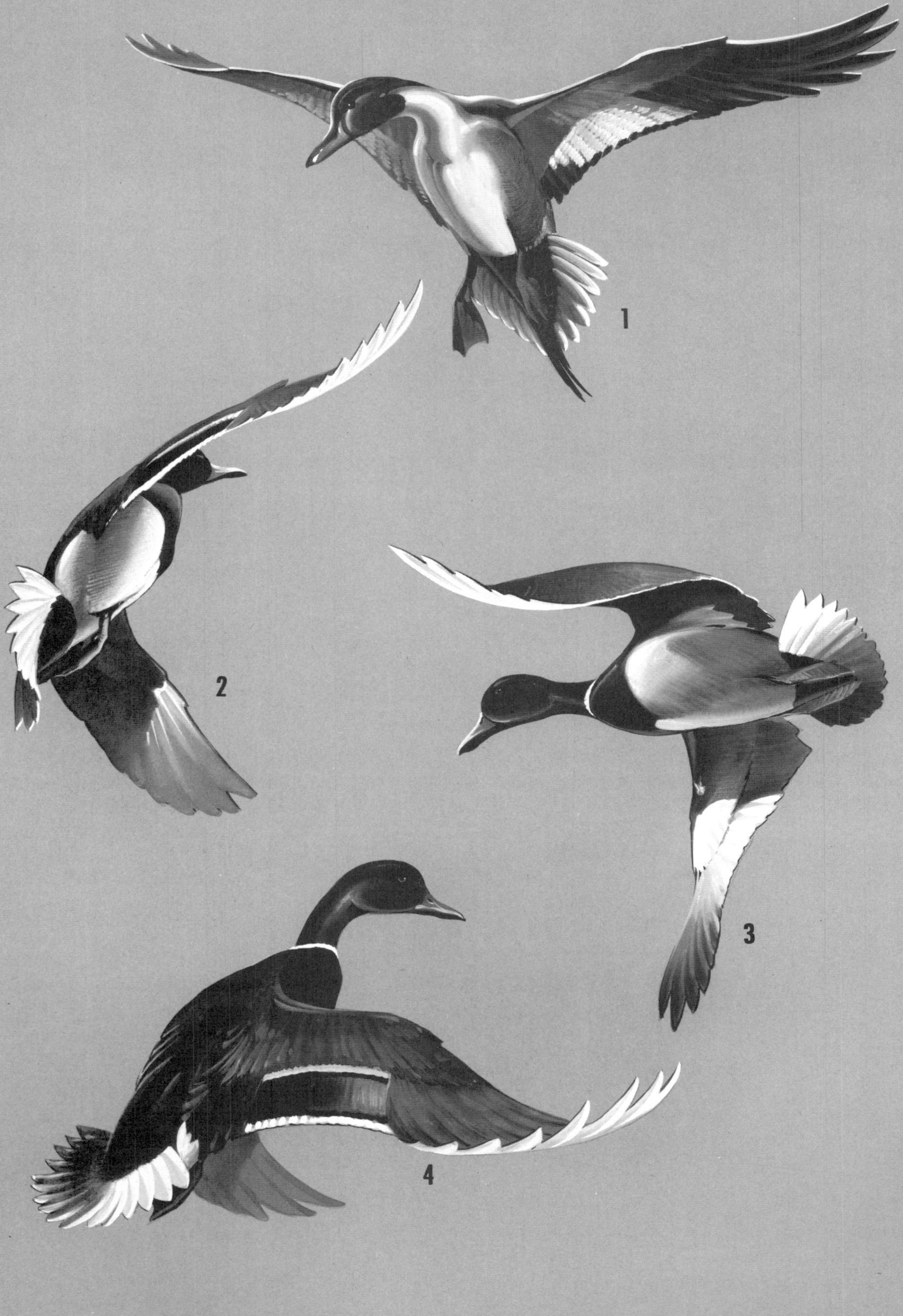

BIRD TAILS AND AERODYNAMICS

The purpose of a bird's tail is to help maintain stability and balance in flight and to assist the wings in changing the bird's forward direction. Depending on the species, a tail consists of sixteen to twenty feathers.

The aerodynamics of a tail in the four basic directions — to the right, left, upward, and downward — are illustrated.

Figure 1 shows a duck preparing to land, the tail depressed and cupped.

Figure 2 illustrates a climbing turn to the left, the tail twisted to create a drag, which in turn swings the body to the left.

Figure 3 shows a turn to the right, the tail raised high on the left in order to steer the body to the right.

Figure 4 shows a climbing flight, the tail turned upward helps force the body into a climbing attitude.

When drawing tails be sure to have the feathers radiate from a common center point.

A few of the many varieties of bird tails are illustrated. The feathers always grow in pairs.

Pileated
Woodpecker

Barn
Swallow

Ruffed
Grouse

Mourning Dove

Ring-necked Pheasant

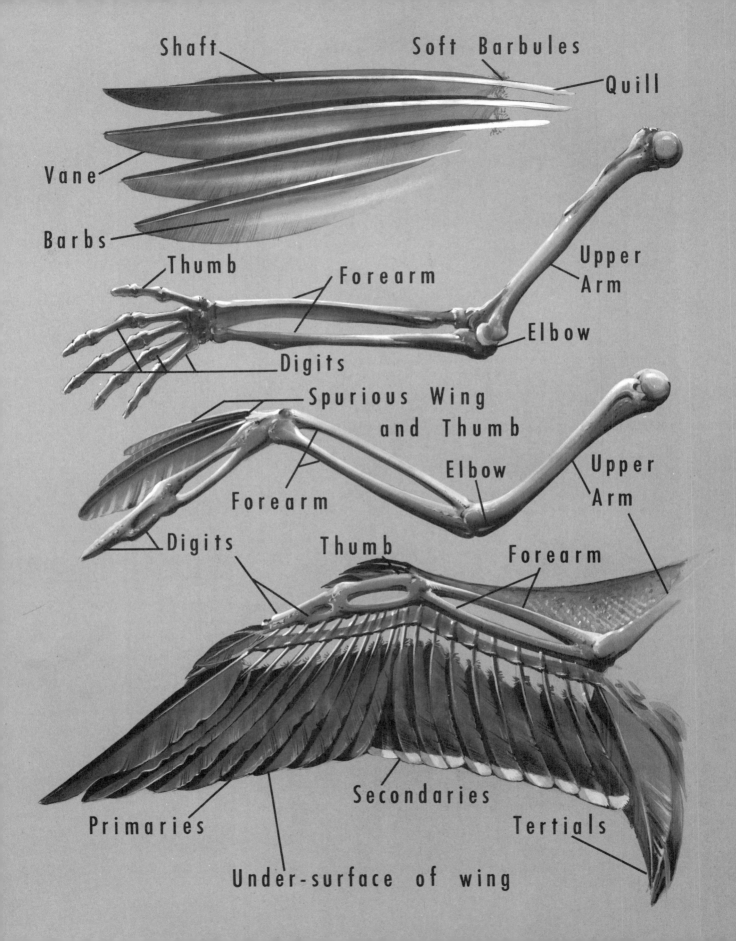

Shaft

Soft Barbules

Quill

Vane

Upper
Arm

Barbs

Thumb

Forearm

Elbow

Digits

Spurious Wing
and Thumb

Elbow

Upper
Arm

Forearm

Forearm

Digits

Thumb

Forearm

Primaries

Secondaries

Tertials

Under-surface of wing

THE ANATOMY OF A WING

The wing of a bird consists of many parts which, combined, form an instrument of flight. If an artist understands how a wing is constructed, the task of drawing one will seem easier.

Comparing bones of the human arm and hand with the wing bones of a wild turkey we find that the main difference is at the tip of the wing. The upper arm and forearm are about the same in appearance.

The wrist joint of the wing remains the same, and what would normally be the thumb section of the human hand has kept the stump of the thumb and added the spurious wing or winglet to the bird's hand. This spurious wing is the vestigial evidence of what was once three claws which archaeornis, a prehistoric reptile-like bird, used for climbing.

What would be the first two fingers or digits of the human hand and the stump of the thumb are fused into a single bone at the tip of the wing bones. The long flight feathers, called *primaries,* attach to this bone.

Next to the primaries are a group of feathers known as the *secondaries.* These feathers attach to the forearm bone (ulna) and support the bird in the air. These are the flight feathers of the inner portion of the wing. Next to the secondaries are the tertials which arise from the upper armbone (humerus) and their main role is to close the gap between the wing and the body.

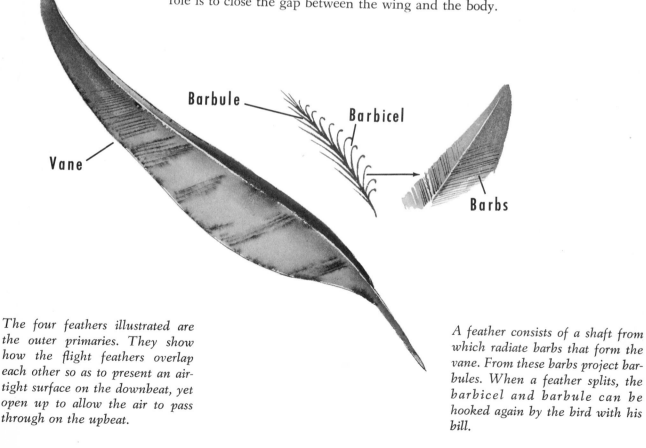

Barbule

Barbicel

Vane

Barbs

The four feathers illustrated are the outer primaries. They show how the flight feathers overlap each other so as to present an airtight surface on the downbeat, yet open up to allow the air to pass through on the upbeat.

A feather consists of a shaft from which radiate barbs that form the vane. From these barbs project barbules. When a feather splits, the barbicel and barbule can be hooked again by the bird with his bill.

Coverts

Primary
Covert

Top View

Primaries

Secondaries Speculum

Tertials

Under View

Wing Lining

1   2   3   4

Folding of a wing

To complete the upper-wing shape nature covers the shaft ends of the primaries with a grouping of feathers called the *primary coverts*. The upper-wing coverts cover a portion of the primary feathers and extend from the spurious wing area to the scapular portion of the body. They streamline the leading edge of the wing and protect the shaft ends of the tertials.

The ends of the under-wing flight feathers are protected by a grouping of feathers called the wing lining. These feathers are similar to the coverts of the upper-wing, and perform the same duty.

THE FOLDING OF A WING

The folding of a bird's wing is quite simple in action. It consists of approximately four basic motions.

Figure 1. As the bird begins the process of folding its wings from an extended position, the primaries are pulled toward the body so that they will pass underneath the secondaries.

Figure 2. As the primaries are passing under the secondaries, the inner portion of the wing or secondaries in turn pass underneath the tertials as the wing continues to fold.

Figure 3. Upon completion of the folding process, the wing is drawn in and held tightly to the sides of the body. With the wings in this position the speculum or chevron, a patch of iridescent color on the secondaries of most ducks, is clearly visible.

Figure 4. To complete the folding action, the tertials are covered with a grouping of feathers known as the *scapulars*. These feathers are located directly over the shoulder blades. Their purpose is to help streamline the wings to the body shape, and to protect the opening between the folded wings and the body from the weather.

These drawings, illustrating the folding, top and under view of a wing, are of the male gadwall duck. Be sure to draw the curvatures of a wing full enough — as shown in the sketch.

SIMPLIFIED WING ACTION

The bird has many wing actions that are quite involved, depending on whether it is gliding, soaring, hovering, diving, taking off, climbing, landing, or in cruising flight. To illustrate a basic wing action, the above drawing is used in place of a complicated, lengthy description of the aerodynamics of flight. It is taken from a movie of a brown pelican.

The pelican has a slow wing beat and its action is easily seen. The wing beat is approximately one and a quarter strokes a second in contrast to a hummingbird's two hundred a second. The bird was in a cruising flight and beginning a slight right turn. The direction of the wing action is indicated by arrows.

Figure 1. Wing in the early phase of the downbeat.
Figure 2. Wing stretched out full, pushing downward and backward.
Figure 3. The wrist joint and inner wing snap upward, followed by the primaries in preparation for the next wing beat.
Figure 4. Wings have reached the top of the arc of the up beat.
Figure 5. Wing thrust is downward with the beginning of the turn.
Figure 6. Wing beat completed, the wrist and inner wing in upward movement.
Figure 7. Primaries snap upward in position for the downbeat.
Figure 8. Wing halfway through the downbeat.

COLOR ON FEATHERS

The various colors seen in a bird's feathers are produced by three different means. The first are the pigmentary colors, which are red, orange, brown, yellow, and grey. The second are the structural colors, which are iridescent green, blue, bronze, and violet. The third form of color is the combination of the pigmented and structural colors.

The drawing shows the construction of a feather through a barb of a secondary feather. These are the speculum feathers and are colorless. They are made up of reflective cells or prisms in the barbs and barbules. The arrangement of these cells in the speculum of a bird's wing break up the light rays into the brilliant iridescent colors.

An accurate control of values is necessary to give the effect of iridescence in a painting.

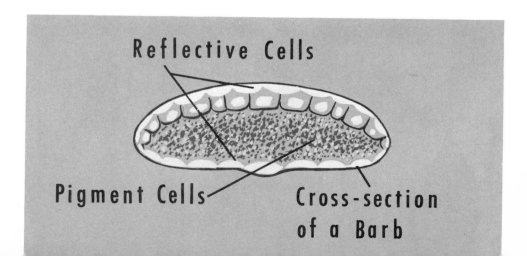

Reflective Cells

Pigment Cells

Cross-section of a Barb

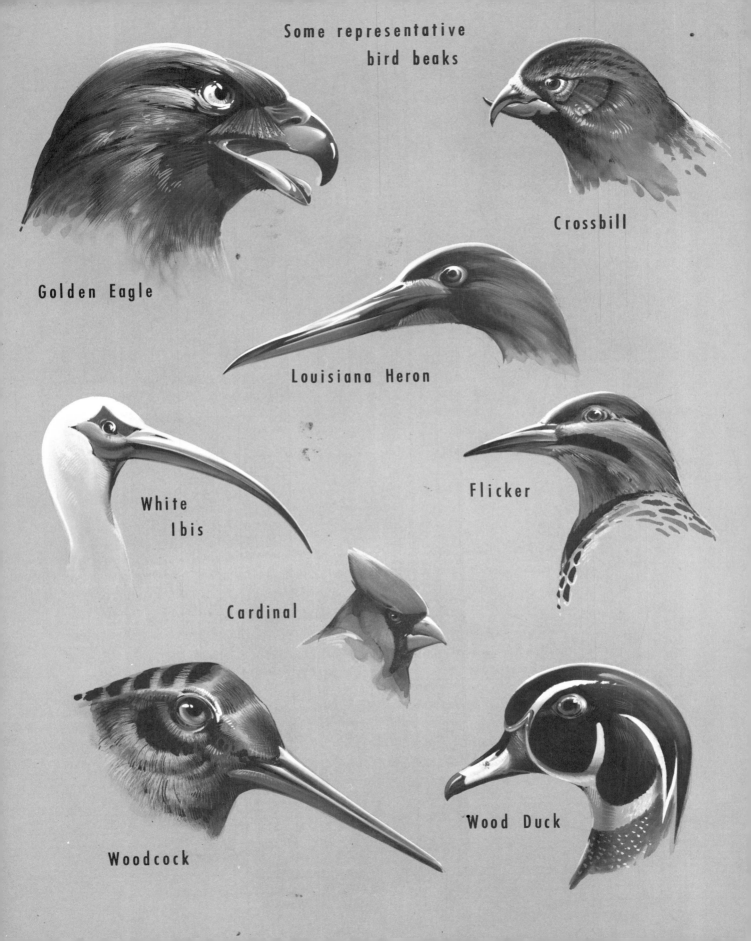

Some representative
bird beaks

Crossbill

Golden Eagle

Louisiana Heron

White
Ibis

Flicker

Cardinal

Woodcock

Wood Duck

REPRESENTATIVE BIRD BILLS

The bill, beak, or upper and lower mandibles, whichever name is preferred, is found in a wide variety of shapes and forms. Nature has designed and adapted each bill for a specialized purpose. The bird's food and feeding habits dictate the shape and form of the bill.

Great care must be exercised by the artist not to understate the proportion and structure of a bill. The beak should be drawn, even though it is of a horny substance, so that it appears to be a continuation of the skull form and not appear glued to the head. The accompanying plate illustrates just a few of the many varieties.

An important point to remember when drawing the bill is to maintain a rhythmic and flowing line as shown in the sketch below.

The various examples of bird beaks were drawn lightly on a grey paper with a 2B pencil, then the forms were put in with simple washes of lampblack. The accents were done with pastel and opaque whites. The values are kept very simple — almost a poster effect in treatment.

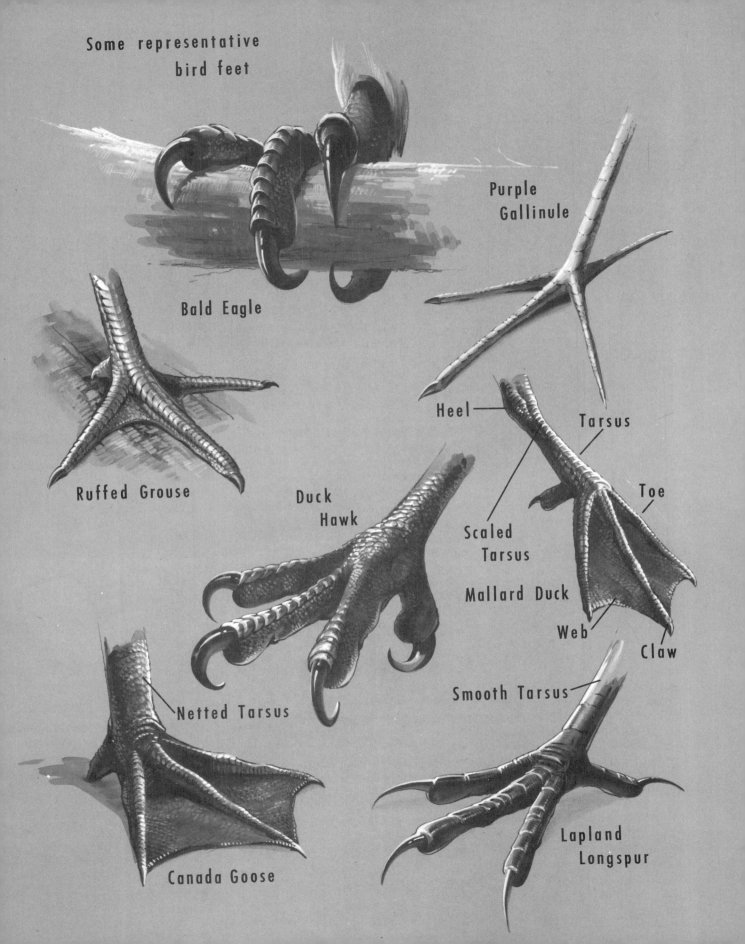

Some representative bird feet

Bald Eagle

Purple Gallinule

Ruffed Grouse

Duck Hawk

Heel

Scaled Tarsus

Tarsus

Toe

Mallard Duck

Web

Claw

Netted Tarsus

Smooth Tarsus

Canada Goose

Lapland Longspur

THE FEET AND THEIR USES

The feet of a bird are important in a drawing. Designed by nature to perform vital functions, they often are passed over lightly in a drawing. The feet of waterfowl, for example, are threefold in their use. On the ground they serve as a means of balance and locomotion. In the water they are used for swimming and paddling about the reeds and grasses. They also assist some types of birds in obtaining flying speed; for example, the underwater feeding ducks which, because of their small wing areas, have to run across the surface of the water to gain flying speed.

In the air the feet serve as a balancing and directional unit. This assist during flight is obtained by opening and closing the feet to create a resistance to the air stream. To illustrate, a bird turning to the right would drop the right wing to create a drag, and raise the left wing to reduce the resistance on that side; then it would open its right foot to increase the resistance and keep the left foot closed. The tail also would act as a rudder during this maneuver. In this manner the bird actually drags itself around a sharp turn.

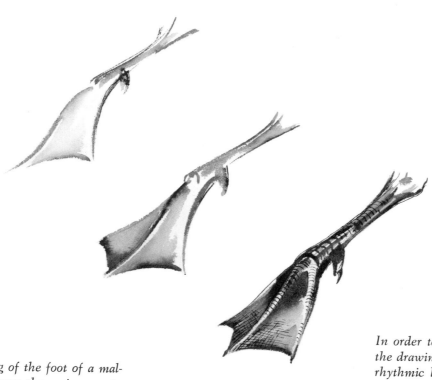

The drawing of the foot of a mallard duck shows the various parts. The arrangement of the joints is as follows: the inside toe has two joints, the middle has three, and the outside has four. The rear toe has only one joint.

In order to put spring and life in the drawing of birds' feet, a strong rhythmic line must be first established, then painted with simple values. If possible the texture should be shown in the middletone values so there will not be an excess of detail. Too much detail weakens the action.

33

CLAY MODELS AND THEIR USE

If the artist will take a few moments and model a simplified bird with cardboard wings and tail, and use this to *see* rather than *guess* the form, foreshortening, or shadows cast, a lot of valuable time will be saved.

Sketch a pair of wings, with their speculums indicated, on a piece of Bristol board and cut them out. Model the body and head of the bird and mount this upon a support. Insert the wings into position and bend to the desired action. Adjust a light source for the required shadows and lighting, and your model is ready for drawing.

To help clarify the wing and tail feather directions and their areas, the cutouts for the model may be carried a step farther by completing them in watercolor as shown.

For a temporary model there are many brands of modeling clay available that do not harden. However, by using clays that do harden you can build up a permanent collection of models.

When painting birds in groups or flocks it is imperative that a simple value treatment be maintained.

AERIAL PERSPECTIVE

When the problem of aerial perspective presents itself and it is not possible to use landscape to assist in creating the illusion of depth, the artist must pay attention to composition, values, and the use of details.

The above drawing will be used to illustrate this. The first aid is the use of white values. There are three different values of white in the drawing. The farthermost bird was made with a thin wash of opaque white and some white pencil accents. For the middle bird an opaque white wash was used, plus minor accents of white pastel, while the nearest bird has a generous use of opaque white wash and white pastel.

The next valuable aids are the progressive uses of feather and eye details. The nearest bird has the details drawn in; in the next, the position of the eye is indicated, and feather direction and contour designated; while in the last, the eye position and feathers are only shown vaguely.

The inverted arc formed by the wing tips consists of three dark values. The distant wing tip is a dark grey, the next a solid lampblack, and the nearest wing tips are a soft carbon pencil over a solid lampblack. The overlapping design of the three birds and their reduction in scale to each other complete the illusion of aerial depth.

35

Progressive Flight—
from 8mm Movie Film

The sketches are of Wilson's snipe, a bird whose flight is so rapid that the wing action would be very difficult to photograph unless a specialized camera was used.

THE CAMERA AND ITS APPLICATION TO WILDLIFE ART

The simplified drawing of a red-tailed hawk in flight was made from an 8-mm. movie film to illustrate the practical use of the camera as an aid in the study of wildlife and their movements. Camera equipment is as necessary to the wildlife artist as his pencils, paints, and brushes.

The fast gait of an animal or the rapid wingbeat of a bird is too quick to perceive and analyze. The camera has proved valuable in capturing these movements, as well as wave motions, waterfalls, and cascades. A fast film will freeze the action so that construction and forms may be studied under ideal conditions in the studio.

Drawn from a movie film, the principle of flight and the sequence of wing, tail, and body actions were made easier to understand by projecting the film at a slow speed and repeating it over and over again.

The reasons given for the application of the camera to art do not mean that an artist is to give up sketching in the field. If an artist depends too much upon the camera for recording information when a sketch will do the job, it may in time prove injurious to his drawing ability. Artistic and drawing ability must remain uppermost. The camera cannot replace human emotions, but it is to be considered as a study aid and for recording facts and details for later reference.

There are some color films that enhance the reds while others accent the blues more than the natural landscape colors. However, if an artist is aware of these limitations, they can be adjusted in the painting.

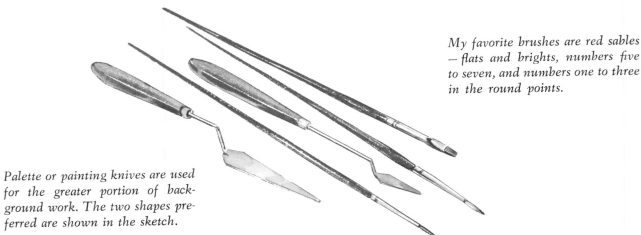

My favorite brushes are red sables — flats and brights, numbers five to seven, and numbers one to three in the round points.

Palette or painting knives are used for the greater portion of background work. The two shapes preferred are shown in the sketch.

PALETTE

For a palette, I prefer plywood with acetate mounted to it. On top of a piece of plywood place a duplicate of the paper or canvas that the picture will be painted upon. To this surface tape a piece of acetate. This makes a clean palette upon which to mix the colors.

The theory is that the colors should be mixed upon a duplicate of the surface on which the picture will be painted and not against a foreign background. To clean, remove the acetate, roll it up and dispose of it. Tape on new acetate and the palette is ready for the next painting.

A BIRD PAINTING—FROM START TO FINISH

The concept of the scene depicted in the demonstration painting originated from a duck hunting trip on the lower reaches and tidal flats of the Myakka River near Sarasota, Florida.

The purpose of this painting is to show the step-by-step procedure in the production of a bird painting. The ring-necked duck in its winter habitat provides the subject matter. This species is seen in this area during the winter migration.

The main interest is centered on the flying birds silhouetted against the sky, while the ducks resting on the water in the immediate foreground play a supporting role in the composition. Landscape does not have a primary part in the scene, so it is subdued in design and color. Since the foliage is quite dry during this season, the burnt oranges, red-violets, and browns predominate.

The first important step is to start composing the abstract design, simplifying the areas to geometric shapes, then gradually developing them into a more realistic form, adding the details of the birds later. In the final picture, the action of foliage has been purposely minimized in order to accent the forward motion of the birds.

Hundreds of ducks were rafted in the lee of some mangroves. From this a few were constantly leaving and flying up and down the river.

ABSTRACT DESIGN

Too often the critical abstract designing of an area is passed over lightly in the haste to get to the final painting. Good abstraction of a projected picture is important and should not be executed hurriedly.

If a design is not pleasing in an arrangement of abstract forms, one certainly cannot expect it to be satisfactory in the final painting.

The first graphic impression of the scene to be painted is kept very simple. Two values of grey, black, and a white are sufficient for the first abstraction.

The first design illustrated was made on grey paper using a wash of lampblack, white chalk, and a felt pen. The second is a further refinement with a definite perspective established.

A felt pen, lampblack for simple washes, opaque white or white pastel on grey paper are excellent mediums when searching for a suitable abstract design.

The third design, which is 3½″ high by 4⅜″ wide, has the forms of the ducks, trees, and grass-like shapes indicated. With a basic perspective and values established, it is ready to be enlarged to a convenient size for layout purpose.

By this time, a complete picture has been well established so that there should be no doubt as to how the next step, which is the color layout, will appear.

THE COLOR SKETCH OR LAYOUT

The design is enlarged at this time. The measurements are doubled so that the picture is 7½″ high by 10″ wide. At this stage, the values of the abstract will be transposed into color. Since the final painting is to be in oil, the layout or color sketch should also be in the same medium.

The working procedure for the advanced phase is as follows: trace the enlarged design onto a piece of illustration board or other suitable surface; after the outlines of the drawing have been transferred and newly penciled, the surface is sprayed with a retouch varnish. This protects the pencil lines and seals the surface. The simplified color palette used was Mars violet, manganese blue, raw sienna, cobalt blue, Naples yellow, and titanium white. The vehicle was Taubes copal painting medium.

The colors and forms are kept quite simple to preserve the abstract or poster quality.

This preliminary work takes time, but in the final analysis the painting will be better for its having been done.

INDIVIDUAL BIRD STUDIES

In order to understand thoroughly the forms of the birds that are to be painted, and to be certain of their flight and wing positions, it has been necessary to make these individual studies. These sketches were quickly drawn, using grey paper, lampblack, and opaque white washes, with accents of carbon pencil and white chalk.

In this study the identifying field marks of the birds are indicated with their lights and shadows. To be certain that the water lies flat, a perspective grid should be drawn. This forms a platform upon which to establish the reflections of the ducks and the ripples on the water surface created by them. This study consists of three drawings combined into one.

DETAIL AND VALUE STUDY

The pencil drawing completes the progressive studies that are made before the final painting is begun. The details that fulfill the landscape design and establish the values are added at this time. A tracing of this value study is made and then transferred to the surface upon which the picture is to be painted.

This pencil drawing value study is on a piece of plate-finish Strathmore board which normally is used for ink drawings. The surface of this paper permits finer values and does not have too much grain with which to contend. This drawing is the same size as the completed oil painting, 10″ high by 14″ wide.

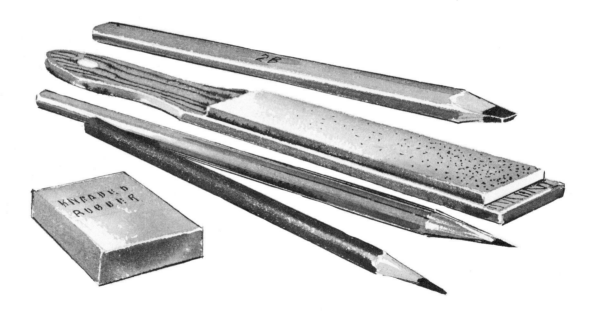

The pencils used are General's sketching pencil (chisel edge), Eberhard Faber "Ebony" layout pencil; 2H, HB, and 2B drawing pencils. A kneaded eraser and sandpaper block are necessary. The drawing is sprayed with an acrolitic fixative when completed.

These pencil drawings should be completed at one sitting, if possible, to maintain a continuity of design.

The time necessary to make this value study is well spent since it helps clarify the forms in relation to each other. It also allows more attention to be given to the technique and *paint* quality of the picture.

When this phase of the progressive steps to the completed painting has been reached, most of the problems concerning the design, values, colors, and the technicalities of the bird species being illustrated have been solved.

It will be noted that in the final painting a few of the ducks on the water have been eliminated as they seemed to draw attention away from the flying birds.

TEMPERA UNDERPAINTING

A simplified tracing is made of the penciled value study and transferred to a piece of illustration board or a painting surface of your choice, in preparation for the final painting. A heavy mounted watercolor board has proved quite ideal for me as a surface upon which to paint.

After the tracing has been transferred, the outlines should be sharpened with a pencil, particularly details of the birds' heads, feet, and the edges of the wing feathers where they overlap.

Once this is completed, the whole surface should be sprayed lightly with a retouch varnish to seal the surface from the oils, and to prevent pencil lines from smudging.

The next step, once the retouch varnish is dry, is to paint in the color areas with egg tempera. For this, dry colors are used with an egg-oil emulsion. At times I mix my own emulsion but generally the prepared form is used. The formula for my own emulsion is as follows — 1 volume of egg yolk, 1 volume of stand oil, 1 volume of damar varnish, and 2 or 3 volumes of water. Shake well and keep refrigerated.

The dry color palette for the underpainting is as follows —
alizarine crimson
cadmium red, medium
cerulean blue
cobalt blue
phthalocyanine green
chromium oxide green opaque
yellow ochre
Naples yellow
burnt sienna
raw umber
burnt umber
titanium white

This picture was made at the completion of the egg-oil tempera underpainting, before the final oil painting was started.

UNDERPAINTING

The underpainting approach that has proved best for me is to limit the painting of the designed areas to not over two or three values. The theory is to paint in a light and dark side, or when rounded forms are present, to introduce a third value, light, middletone, and dark values only.

With this approach to underpainting, the masses of the abstract design still have been preserved until the final phase of the painting. Blending or modeling of forms and the glazing will be executed in the oil portion of the painting whenever possible. The color pattern of the wings of the third duck in the flight group, in this particular painting, dictated that some modeling would be necessary, but usually blending is to be avoided whenever possible in the underpainting.

47

The above details are actual size and show the handling of the oil-wax medium, and the palette knife and brush combination.

OIL PAINTING

With the completion of the egg-oil tempera underpainting the medium is then changed to an oil and wax technique. The palette used for this painting is as follows: Naples yellow, barium yellow, viridian, chromium oxide green opaque, cobalt blue, manganese blue, alizarine crimson, vermilion, transparent golden ochre, raw sienna, burnt umber, raw umber, Mars violet, titanium white, and Dorland's wax medium combined with Taubes copal painting medium.

During the early phase of the oil painting, forms are kept very simple, usually to a light, middletone, dark, and a reflected light, without too much blending of values. The intermediate stage consists of adding the secondary forms, development and enriching of colors, and a soft blending of forms where required. The matt areas are intensified with light sprayings of retouch varnish.

During the last stage of the painting, minute details such as high lights of the eyes, various spots of color, and leaf forms in the landscape are completed. The blues are intensified by glazing to complement the various oranges in the landscape, and also to simplify the color pattern of the water, since it is broken by reeds and grasses. The red-browns are also neutralized with a soft glaze of green. The glaze used consists mainly of wax and very little pigment, thinned with copal painting medium.

When all of the details and various glazes are completed and are thoroughly dry, the painting is then given a thin coat of wax to eliminate the glare created by the varnishes, and to form a protective coating for the painting.

Ring-necks on the Myakka

Oil on illustration board (14″ by 10″)

FISH

A study of the problems involved in drawing and painting fish, their anatomy and proportions, and a progressive demonstration of a painting from the original abstract to the completed work.

SECTION II.

Dolphin swimming among honey-combed rock and seaweed — an example of a design originating from sea life.

Sketched from a Minoan jug, circa 1600 B.C.

APPROACH TO FISH ILLUSTRATION

With the growth of skin diving as a sport, interest in the sea and its many species of fish, their lives and habitat, has reached major proportions. The color and beauty of the underwater world has been unveiled by adventurous skin diving artists, naturalists, and photographers. Previously one had to imagine how it appeared under the surface of the sea, but now there are clear, concise pictures and illustrations.

With this research available, the artist is able to design and paint authentic scenes and backgrounds for marine portraits and illustrations. In order to simplify the task of describing and explaining problems in drawing and painting fish, it is necessary to concentrate on only a few species. As the fresh-water fish is more familiar to most of us than salt-water species, they will serve as a basis upon which to concentrate our study efforts.

The great barracuda, a dweller of the outer reefs, commonly known as the Tiger of the Sea, has earned its reputation for cruelty and voracious attacks. This drawing was made with washes of lampblack, opaque greys and whites, and pastel grey pencils on a grey paper.

TECHNICALITIES OF WILDLIFE ART

A question often asked is whether technical knowledge is a necessity in order to paint a wildlife subject successfully. In order to study, describe or understand some of the problems, it is desirable to know something of the language. To speak of the snout, head, mandible, or dorsal fin of a fish is no different than to discuss the nose, head, lower jaw or back, of the human body. These descriptive terms assist in locating areas used for identification.

Fortunately, most commonly known fish can be classified into a few families, species, and sub-species. Great care should be exercised when painting a representative portrait of a species that it shows a true member and not a lesser known one by error.

The drawing is used to illustrate this point. The fish in the upper left is probably the best known and most widely distributed of the rainbow trout. It is a McCloud River rainbow, an excellent specimen of the species; but the heavily spotted fish is also a rainbow, although it is of the lesser known type. This is the Kern River rainbow. Therefore, the McCloud River rainbow should be the preferred one to paint.

Topography of a Fish
(Eastern Brook Trout)

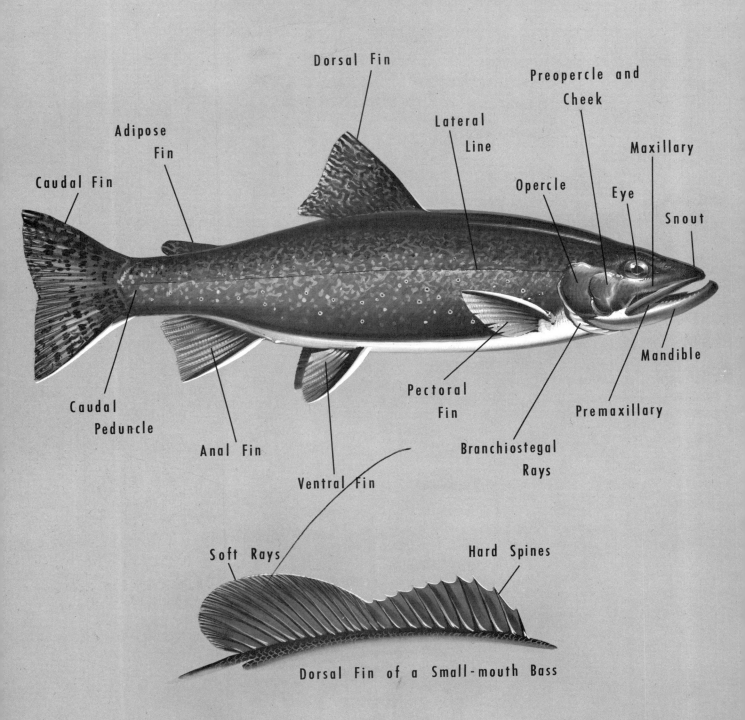

Dorsal Fin

Preopercle and Cheek

Lateral Line

Maxillary

Adipose Fin

Caudal Fin

Opercle

Eye

Snout

Caudal Peduncle

Pectoral Fin

Mandible

Anal Fin

Branchiostegal Rays

Premaxillary

Ventral Fin

Soft Rays

Hard Spines

Dorsal Fin of a Small-mouth Bass

TOPOGRAPHY OF A FISH

Since there are hundreds of varieties of fish found in fresh and salt water, it would not be practical to discuss each form. In order to show the topography of a fish and some additional variations, the eastern brook trout will serve as the model for the fresh-water fish, while on the following page, the Atlantic sailfish and bonito will be models for the salt-water species.

SNOUT — part of a fish's head that projects forward and contains the nose and the upper and lower jaws.

MAXILLARY or MAXILLA — upper jaw.

MANDIBLE — lower jaw.

PREMAXILLARY — bones or plates on both sides of the maxillary that form the front portion of the upper jaw.

EYE — organ of sight or vision.

PREOPERCLE and CHEEK — the bony, plate-like form in front of the opercle and usually parallel to it.

OPERCLE — gill cover; the bony membrane that covers the gill opening.

BRANCHIOSTEGAL RAYS — bony rays that support the membrane, under the head and behind the lower jaw.

PECTORAL FIN — uppermost anterior fins. These fins are in pairs.

LATERAL LINE — a series of mucus secreting tubes that form a raised line along the outer sides of a fish.

DORSAL FIN — the fin on the back. This fin is found in many forms and may consist of hard spines and soft rays or only of soft rays.

VENTRAL FIN — paired fins, usually below and behind the pectoral fins.

ADIPOSE FIN — a fleshy, fin-like projection located on the posterior section of the back.

ANAL FIN — the fin on the center line of a fish, located in back of the vent.

CAUDAL PEDUNCLE — posterior section of a fish located between the tail and the anal fin.

HARD SPINES — sharp, projecting points, usually located in the fins.

SOFT RAYS — articulated fin rays that terminate in branchlike forms.

BARBELS — long, fleshy projections found on the head of a fish.

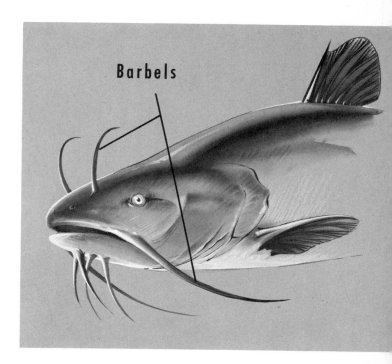

Barbels

The dangerous part of a catfish is the hard spine located in the front section of the dorsal fin.

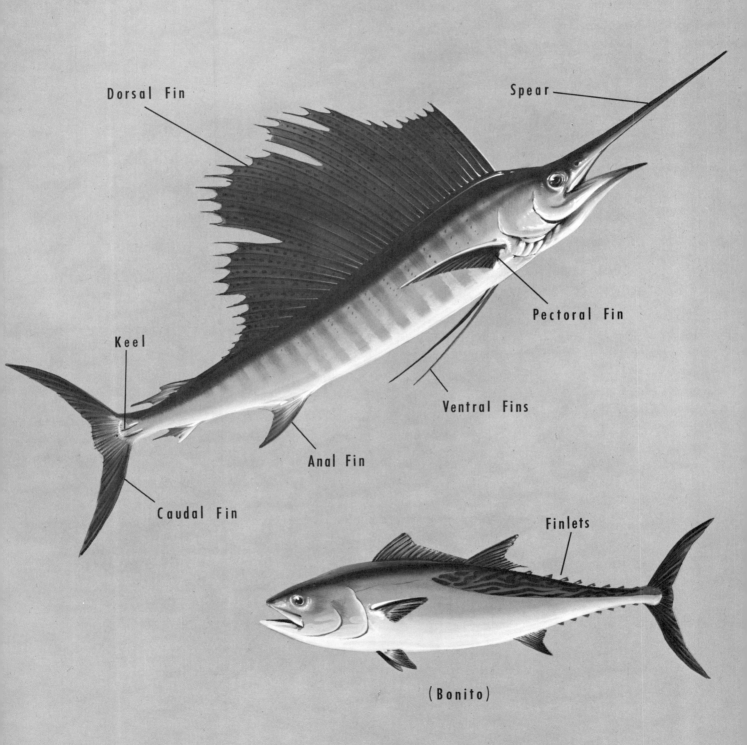

Topography of a Fish
(Sailfish)

Dorsal Fin

Spear

Keel

Pectoral Fin

Ventral Fins

Anal Fin

Caudal Fin

Finlets

(Bonito)

SPEAR — an extension of the maxillary into a long spear or bill.

KEEL — fleshy crests on the caudal peduncle.

FINLETS — small fins located on the median line of the caudal peduncle.

The tarpon's dorsal fin is short at the base. The last ray terminates in a filament-like form.

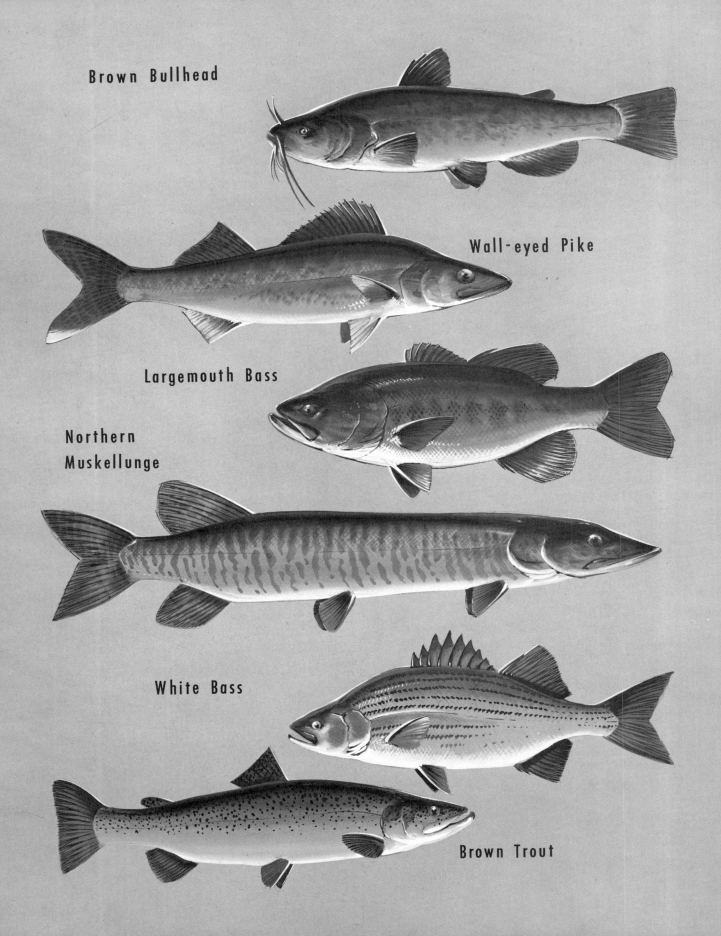

Brown Bullhead

Wall-eyed Pike

Largemouth Bass

Northern
Muskellunge

White Bass

Brown Trout

SPECIES OR FAMILIES OF FISH

The drawings in this section illustrate some of the various *families* of better known fresh-water game fish. To simplify the task, they have been confined to just a few of the popular specimens.

The grouping of families is generally separated by the arrangement of the fins, the silhouette, and the color pattern. A further breakdown of the species within the family of fish necessitates a finer classification.

The various categories shown are, from top to bottom, the *catfish, perch, sunfish, pike,* the *bass* and *salmon*. Comparing the drawing of the fish with the order just given, it is evident that the bullhead is a member of the *catfish* family; the wall-eyed pike is not a pike but belongs to the *perch* family. The largemouth bass is a member of the *sunfish* family, while the muskellunge is grouped with the *pikes*. The white bass is a true bass, and the brown trout is a member of the *salmon* family.

The grouping with the largest breakdown of fresh-water species and sub-species are the *sunfish* and *salmon* families.

The hogfish, a salt-water fish, is a member of the wrasses, *which includes many species. There are few gamefish in this group.*

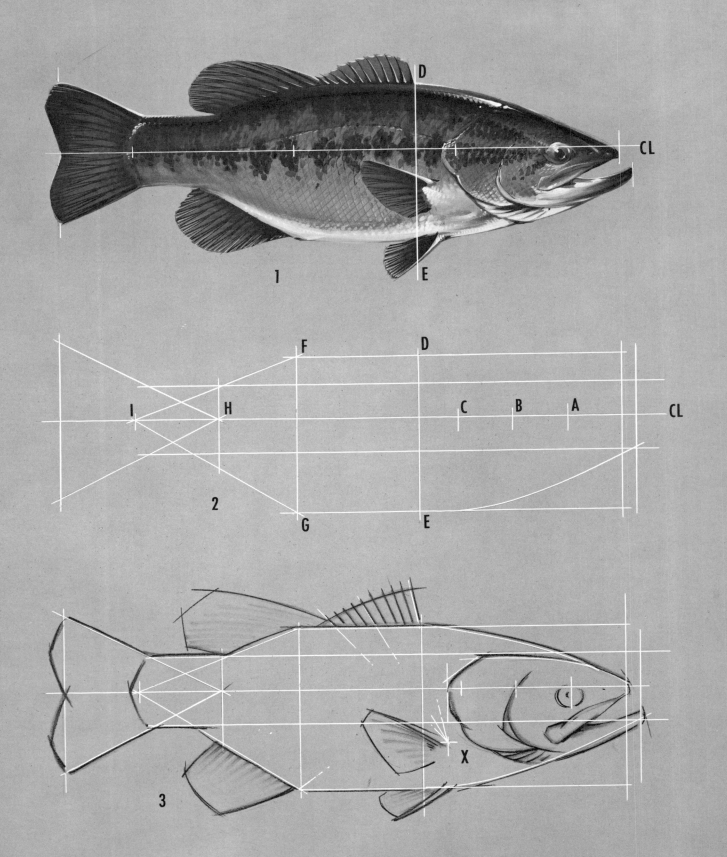

1

D

CL

E

2

F   D

I   H   C   B   A   CL

G   E

3

X

MATHEMATICAL AND GEOMETRIC FORMS

One of the valuable aids to the artist is the mathematical and geometric division of a fish. In drawing the human figure, the length of the head has been established as a unit of measure. When drawing fish in perspective, the body forms are simplified into a few geometric shapes and a unit of measure developed.

By establishing a vertical line (DE) from the front of the dorsal fin to the belly line, a length of measure is developed which can be used as a *unit of measure*. Once this unit, which I call the dorsal line of measure (DLM), has been established, it is used to measure the length of the fish along the center line (CL).

The average divisions usually fall into thirds and fourths from the snout to the end of the caudal peduncle. The letters A, B, and C divide the head into thirds. The first third (A) from the snout to the eye, the second (B) from the eye to the back portion of the preopercle, and the last third (C) from the preopercle to the posterior section of the opercle.

The apex of the triangular shape of the opened tail (H) is usually in the middle of the last unit of measure of the body. In some instances the hard spines radiate from a point (X) near the root of the pectoral fin.

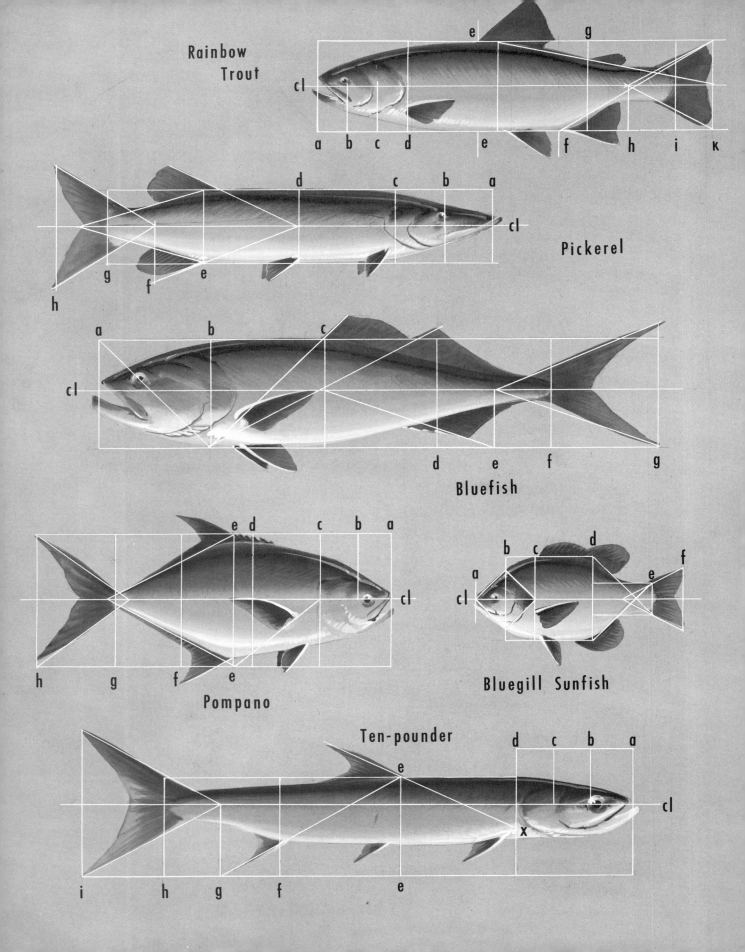

Rainbow Trout

Pickerel

Bluefish

Pompano

Bluegill Sunfish

Ten-pounder

EXAMPLES OF THE DORSAL LINE OF MEASUREMENT

To help clarify and illustrate the application of a means of measuring with the *dorsal line of measurement* (DLM), a few representative fish are shown.

The first model is the rainbow trout. We are only concerned with the contour, so color and patterns are not shown. Line (ee) is the DLM. This unit divides the trout into four divisions. The head is easily divided into equal segments (a, b, c, d). The apex of the tail is at point (h), at the center of the last section.

It will also be noted that the diagonals help in projecting the directions of the back and anal fin lines. Another point to be remembered is that most ventral fin locations are approximately at the halfway or middle point in the length of the body.

The pickerel, a member of the pike family, also divides into four parts, but the eye line is at the halfway mark instead of in the first third of the head division, as explained previously. The triangle which assists in locating the angle of the caudal fin terminates at point (f) and the center line (cl).

The other triangle, terminating on line (d) and the center line (cl), forms the contour for the dorsal and anal fin line.

An interesting combination of the mathematical and geometric divisions is shown in the pompano and bluegill sunfish. These are exceptions to the rule. The rest of the drawings are self-explanatory. The pompano, ten-pounder, and bluefish are salt-water species, while the rainbow, bluegill sunfish, and pickerel are fresh-water types.

CONVERTING GEOMETRIC GRID TO PERSPECTIVE

The task of converting the geometric form of a fish into a perspective grid is fairly simple. The center diagram (drawing #2, page 60) of the large-mouth bass will serve as the model to demonstrate this procedure.

The first drawing on page 64, illustrates the principle of advancing a given area or measurement by the use of diagonal lines, which we should understand before proceeding.

With *bcde* as the given area and cross diagonals establishing its center, we then draw the center line *cl*. From corner *b* through the intersection of lines *cl* and *de,* project a line until it touches a continuation of line *cd*. From this point, *f,* draw a perpendicular to line *be*. This forms an equal area. Repeat the same procedure as many times as needed.

Understanding this principle, we can then convert the grid to a perspective drawing. Take the horizontal line measurements on line *DE* (drawing #2, page 60) and reduce or enlarge them to the desired scale and mark them on line *bc* (drawing #2, page 64). Project these lines to a vanishing point, then estimate the first rectangle *bcde*. Draw the diagonal and repeat three times to establish the length of the fish.

Construct the triangles for the posterior portion of the body and tail. With this form established, it is then a simple procedure to complete the drawing of the fish, as illustrated.

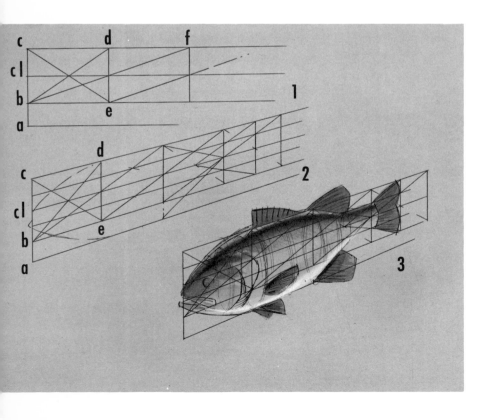

Drawings #1 and #2 are very similar to projecting a fence and its posts, whether in perspective or in a mechanical drawing.

This drawing of a pickerel was made with washes of lampblack and opaque white on grey paper. The dark forms were put in with a carbon pencil. This is a very easy way to make a drawing. The middletone grey is established by the color of the paper, so all that needs to be done is to add the darks and the lights.

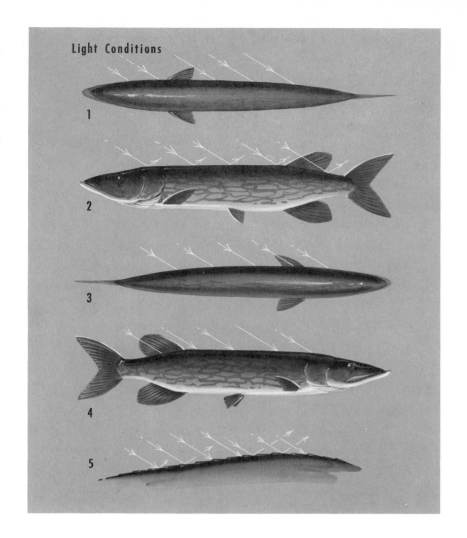

UNDERWATER LIGHT CONDITIONS

A condition that alters the color of fish in *underwater* scenes, is the amount of light reflected or absorbed by the scales. This means that if a fish is swimming away from you, with the light passing into the water to the front and side of the fish (drawings #1 and #2), the local color of the fish will be weakened by the reflected light.

If the fish is swimming toward you and the same light condition exists (drawings #3 and #4), the overlapping of the scales, like the shingles on a roof, will absorb some of the light rays and the color.of the fish will then appear darker.

An enlarged view of the sides of a fish (as illustrated in drawing #5, which is similar to drawing #3), shows that some of the light rays are being reflected while others are being absorbed by the overlapping scales.

REFRACTION AND REFLECTION

There are times when an artist may be required to show the reflection of light and the refraction of objects in water; for example, in an illustration with a view towards the bottom of a pond, a fish as the center of interest, and some grass and branches projecting from the bottom and above the surface of the water.

The artist should know something about the phenomena before attempting to draw it. Refraction occurs when a ray of light, or an object penetrating a clear fluid, is bent from its original course to a more oblique angle to the surface.

Reflection of light or color occurs when the ray is bounced or reflected from a surface onto an object. This is clarified in the illustration. The light ray, as shown by the white lines of the drawing, penetrates the water and is refracted and then reflected from the bottom to the undersides of the fish. Understanding the principles of reflection and refraction simplifies the problem of preserving a realistic appearance in the scene.

Attention to small details, such as reflected light and refraction, adds to the authenticity of a drawing.

The dolphin, Beau Brummell of the deep, is noted for its rapid color changes. Varying combinations of yellow, green, and blue are always present, speckled with a pattern of dark spots.

COLOR AND COLOR CHANGES IN FISH

The color changes and patterns in fish are many and varied. In some species there are known to exist at least seven distinct color patterns. Some of these changes are brought about by such things as fright, anger, fear, environment, seasonal changes or spawning, distress, and the mimicry of other fish or background.

These color movements are the result of the contraction or expansion of color cells that contain the three primaries, yellow, red, and blue. The color cells may also contain, in addition to the primaries, black or some other color pigment.

The movements of color cells are controlled by the nervous system. The stimulus for these movements is received through the optic nerve.

The basic rules of perspective apply to an underwater scene the same as they would to drawing a room.

PERSPECTIVE

In the drawing of the lake trout swimming upward toward the bait, a one-point perspective proved sufficient to focus attention on the fish and to create an illusion of depth in the scene. A perspective grid is valuable in establishing ellipses and also in keeping the water *flat,* not running uphill.

A major difference in an underwater landscape is the appearance and addition of a reflective surface. The under surface or *ceiling* of water reflects images the same as a mirror. Wave action would tend to distort reflected images.

A fish in clear water appears as though it were floating in space. The presence of water is made visible by floating debris and matter. Unless there is a shadow cast from a fish it would be difficult to tell how far it is above the bottom or what distance it is from the observer.

68

PROPORTION, SCALE

A means of establishing the scale, size, or proportion of a fish is by its *comparison* to a common object. In the accompanying illustration of a lake trout, whose weight may be up to twenty pounds, its largeness was achieved by comparison to the small fish and underwater plant life.

The apparent nearness of the fish to the observer also is helpful in creating size. If a fish is small, the psychological effect of looking down on it will accent its smallness. To look directly at or upward toward a subject tends to make it appear larger.

If an artist is painting or drawing a game fish, such as a largemouth bass, for example, an artificial spoon, plug or fly is an excellent comparison to show the size of the fish, or if a common object like a leaf can be introduced to the scene without being too obvious, the scale of the fish is then easily established.

This drawing was made with washes of lampblack, opaque greys, and white on a grey paper. The overall form of the fish was first developed in washes of lampblack and then the spotting was added with the opaque greys.

CLAY MODEL

The use of modeling clay is again applied as a means of solving the perspective, lighting, or foreshortening problems that arise. The support or armature for the model is made from a piece of wire clothes hanger. The wire is bent into shape and covered with masking tape so that the clay will adhere to the frame.

The body of the fish is then modeled on the form and cardboard fins and tail are added to complete it. A single source of light is preferred when studying the contour of the cast shadows.

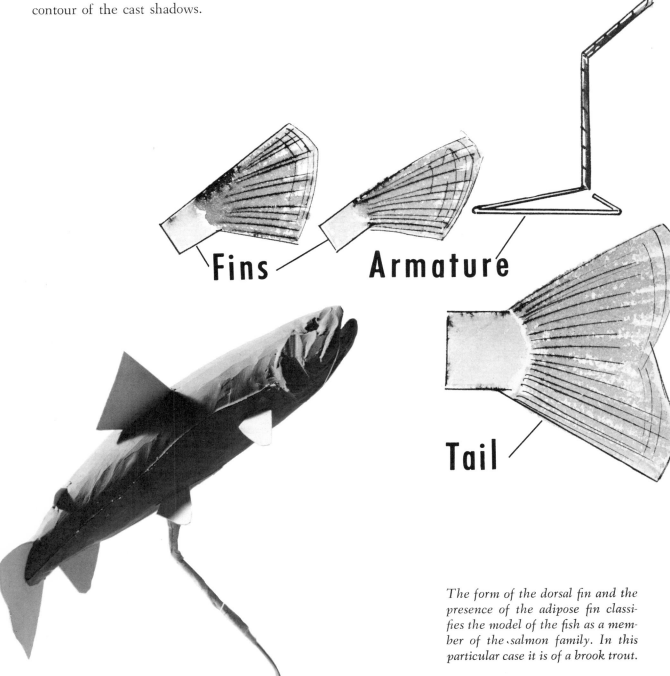

Fins   Armature

Tail

The form of the dorsal fin and the presence of the adipose fin classifies the model of the fish as a member of the ·salmon family. In this particular case it is of a brook trout.

SWIMMING MOVEMENT AND ACTION

The greatest means of locomotion or movement of a fish is created by its tail. The undulation of the tail and the swimming motion of the pectoral fins are its major forms of motion. The dorsal fin, in some species, also assists by creating action with a sideward, to and fro movement.

Artistic license is employed in drawing the action of the dorsal fin of a jumping fish in order to show the fin to its best advantage. A leaping or jumping fish will, at times, keep its dorsal fin depressed. There are exceptions to this rule, but in most cases the fin is kept near the body.

In a painting of a game fish, the artist should also determine the fighting characteristics of the fish in order to portray it accurately. Some game fish when hooked will stay down deep while others prefer to become aerial acrobats. A rainbow trout, for example, will do its fighting on top of the water, while a brown trout prefers to do its fighting deep.

This simplified sketch of a brown trout was made with a wash of lampblack, opaque white, and carbon pencil.

A PAINTING FROM START TO FINISH

The inspiration for this painting, which is to serve as a demonstration piece, is a composite of a nostalgic affection. My fondness for the eastern brook trout developed when, as a boy, I lived in the hills of Pennsylvania. And the background comes from memories of the wonderful cascades and waterfalls seen on trips into the Smokies and the Blue Ridge Mountains of Tennessee and the Carolinas.

When portraying the brook trout, I feel that the spirit of the fish and its living habits have a much more important meaning than a meticulous, detailed painting of the species. The tremendous force and action that is created by water cascading over rocks, and the pool with its swirling currents at its base, form an excellent stage to display the colorful trout.

The above designs are reproduced the same size as the original. Grey paper, felt pen, opaque white, and lampblack washes are the mediums.

ABSTRACT DESIGN

Again the importance of a good abstract design as a preliminary to the final painting is stressed. Good, acceptable art, whether it is for the art critic, artist or the average individual must have a pleasing design, be in good balance, and well adjusted in forms and color.

Once this design is achieved, and it is done through the application of the abstract, the fundamentals of values, perspective, and anatomy, if needed, are introduced.

Until one becomes proficient in design, the constant practice of making small non-objective abstract designs in color, value, and forms is not to be ignored.

73

THE CAMERA AS A WORKING TOOL

The value of the camera as a means of gathering reference material for paintings of fish subjects has proved itself many times. Pictures of this type generally are obtained during vacations, fishing trips or at odd moments that are unplanned. It is not always possible to catch a large bass, for example, when a model is needed, so most material is obtained when the opportunity presents itself, with the chance that it will be useful later. There also are times when it is not convenient to carry sketch material or when time may be short.

My cameras consist of 35-mm. still and 8-mm. movie. The still camera is used in photographing details such as markings, proportions, and contours. When photographing fish for later reference I generally take three pictures, a side view for contour and markings, a top view for contour and thickness, and a front view for head detail. If the body markings are complicated, a close-up is made.

The movie camera is used to photograph local atmosphere, such as a fishing fleet, seascape or landscape, cascades, pools, or whatever the case may be. In general, I use it where detail is not necessary but where props are needed for background. There are occasions when one may be fortunate and get some action shots of jumping fish, but pictures of this type are usually difficult to obtain.

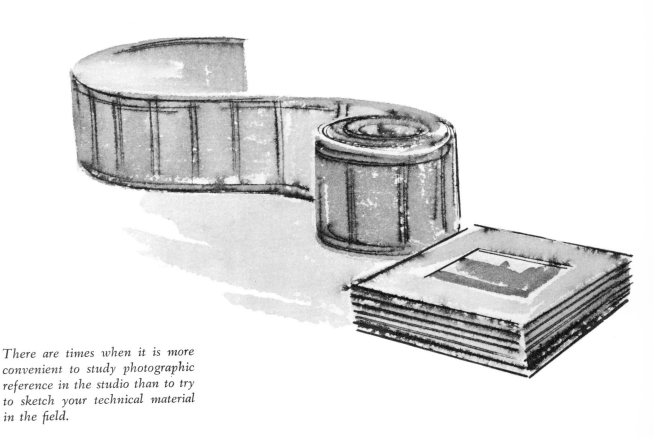

There are times when it is more convenient to study photographic reference in the studio than to try to sketch your technical material in the field.

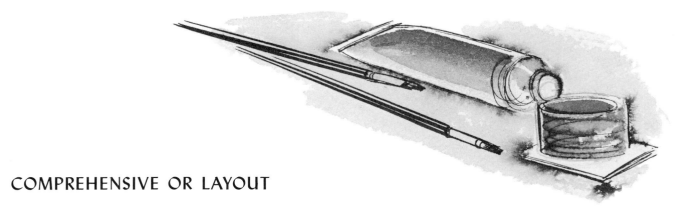

COMPREHENSIVE OR LAYOUT

The layout for *Trout Pool* was painted in oil on an illustration board that had first been sprayed with a retouch varnish. A comprehensive or design should be executed at one sitting and painted quickly in order to capture the spirit of the scene.

The size of the original sketch is 5¾″ high and 7″ wide and it was painted in limited colors. Rose madder, burnt umber, yellow ochre, cobalt, and permanent green deep, plus white, proved sufficient as a palette.

The sketching materials used to make these studies were lampblack and opaque white washes on grey paper, with accents of white pastel.

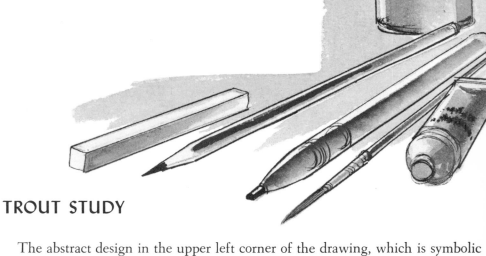

TROUT STUDY

The abstract design in the upper left corner of the drawing, which is symbolic of the leaping fish, was made to assure a strong, rhythmic pattern for the center of interest.

From this abstract, the complete form, with a semblance of some detail, was developed. Once this phase was completed, attention was given to the serpentine design of the dorsal fin and a simplified study of the body markings was indicated.

CASCADE STUDY

To see and realize the destructive force of water, its hidden might as it tears away at earth and rocks, always has had a fascination for me. With this interest I try to include water in the backgrounds of paintings for motion, color, and design whenever possible.

In my files are many feet of movie film of streams, sparkling brooks, cascades, and thunderous waterfalls for reference material and study. Using a movie camera as an aid to art makes it comparatively easy to understand the action of cascading water simply by projecting it at a slow speed and running it over and over until it is thoroughly understood. By this procedure, it is a simple thing to sketch in the design of the water area or action to the composition. In this particular case, I felt that a cascade and a pool with a circular motion was needed to complete the action and form a base for the painting.

This study was made so that the form and action of the cascade was thoroughly understood before attempting to paint it.

COLOR PALETTE AND BRUSHES

Before proceeding with this painting, a limited color palette was decided upon: Shiva burnt umber, alizarine crimson, cadmium green, Shiva blue-light, Permanent Pigments transparent Mars Yellow, and Weber's Permalba white. As the picture progressed, the intermixing of the pigments produced more than enough colors to complete the painting. To these pigments Dorland's wax medium was added, thinned with Taubes copal painting medium.

The greater portion of the painting was executed with red sable flat and bright brushes, numbers five to seven; the fine details were put in with a number one, round point brush. There is a minimum of palette knife used in the turbulent water and foam of the cascade.

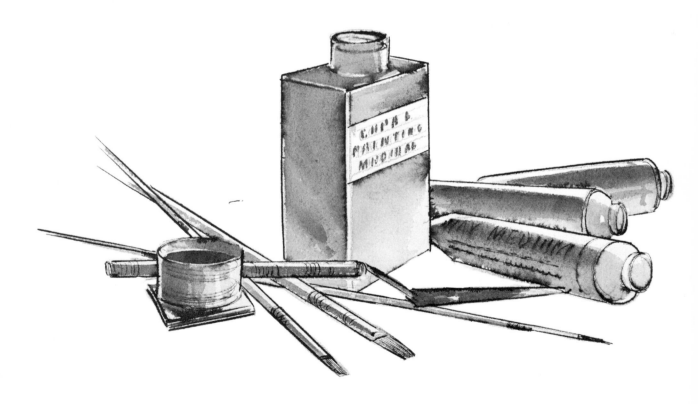

Painting wax and copal medium help the oil paint dry very quickly. This drying time can be slowed by adding a bit of linseed oil.

The original size of this under-painting is 12½" high by 18¼" wide. It was painted on illustration board.

UNDERPAINTING

The painting of the "Trout Pool" is a studio picture and was not sketched at any particular place. The cascade is a variation of a stream in the Blue Ridge Mountains of North Carolina, the trout details are from reference files, and the over-all scene is from imagination.

To change the pace of my working procedure, I decided to dispense with the egg-oil tempera underpainting and use only oil in its place. The overall design was sketched on Strathmore illustration board with a 2B pencil. The surface then was completely covered with a spray of retouch varnish and allowed to dry for a half hour before I began to paint.

79

These enlargements show the brush handling. Each stroke carries the perspective and direction of the form.

OIL PAINTING

Care must be exercised in a picture of this type that it remains a portrait of the fish in its habitat and not a *landscape* with a leaping fish as added interest to the scene.

The picture on the previous page was made at the completion of the under-painting to show the handling of the values. The darks of the rocks were painted first in two values in order to set the key of the painting. The trees were intentionally kept *loose* in treatment to focus attention to the trout, which is handled quite *tight* for detail, and to force the interest to the subject of the painting.

Additional forms were added to the cascade to create more action and help set the mood of the picture. A *blocky* treatment seemed necessary to carry out the movement of the current in the pool and also to create an air of mystery to the depth of the pool.

The cross current, formed by the waterfall to the right of the large rock and the cascade to the left of the rock, with the outlet of the pool behind the tree on the right, holds the center of interest within the picture.

In the order of painting, the rocks were painted first, then the trees, cascade, and pool, with the trout and its details last. When the painting was completely dry, it was coated with a thin covering of Dorland's wax medium, thinned with some copal painting medium, to protect the surface and also to reduce any annoying shine on the picture.

Trout Pool

Oil on illustration board (12½″ by 18¼″)

ANIMALS

The study of the anatomy, form, and actions of an animal, and a progressive demonstration of a painting from the original abstract design to the completed work.

SECTION III.

Reindeer—a facsimile of prehistoric animal art. Circa 15,000 B.C. (Cartillac and Breuil)

APPROACH TO ANIMAL DRAWING AND PAINTING

The study of the anatomy of animals can be greatly simplified by concentrating on a single animal in the beginning, rather than upon many varieties. If one learns as much as possible about a representative animal such as a deer or horse, for example, then that knowledge becomes a guide in the drawing or painting of similar animals. An artist with an understanding of the anatomy of the human body will find the study of animal anatomy easier, since bone and muscular structures are comparatively similar.

Unfortunately for the wildlife artist, wild animals, unless trained, are unlike human models and will not hold a pose on command which, of course, makes them difficult to sketch. A caged animal is easier to draw for details and general conformation, but it lacks the alertness of a creature in the wild where vigilance is always necessary in order to survive.

A difference that can be readily seen between a caged and a wild animal is the condition of the coat or mane. A healthy caged lion will have a full and beautiful mane since it does not have to cope with living conditions in the wild. The mane of a wild lion is usually short, its hairs having been worn or pulled out by brush, fighting, and everyday living.

A rapid action sketch is sufficient for the foundation of an animal painting. Then the anatomy and conformation can be developed from the sketch. At times caged animals will pace a lot. In that event it is better to keep more than one sketch going in order to capture the actions and moods.

Simplicity of line with a slight indication of form is all that is required in the sketching of a moving animal. An animal in repose is easier to draw, and the effort then should be directed toward a study of details, such as eyes, ears, and head. Constant practice soon establishes a systematic approach to sketching animals.

84

These sketches were made on grey paper with washes of lampblack and opaque white. The heavy, black lines were made with an opaque lampblack.

WIRE MANIKIN FOR QUICK ACTION INDICATION

The black lines superimposed over the sketches are the first lines I draw when beginning a sketch of an animal. These lines, which I refer to as the *wire manikin,* carry some indication of the perspective of the animal, its action and rhythm.

Probably the first and most important line is the center line. In the case of the deer sketch the lower neck and back lines are drawn first. The shoulder and rear leg lines are next. The wire manikin quickly establishes the bulk of the animal if the drawing is made to appear transparent.

RHYTHM AND ACTION LINES

One of the most important phases in the beginning of a drawing or painting is the first series of sketches, when action and rhythm are established. As shown in the accompanying sketches, the main action lines tie in with various contour points of the animal so that a rhythmic, flowing or optical line-up of areas or points is achieved.

If a pleasing rhythm has not been accomplished in the sketches when establishing these lines, *do not proceed further* until this has been achieved as it is extremely important to the final success of the painting. There is no set rule to guide you in making these sketches as it is a personal emotion. You will know when the sketch looks right.

Quick sketch of a whitetail deer made with a felt pen, lampblack, and opaque white washes. The action lines are lampblack.

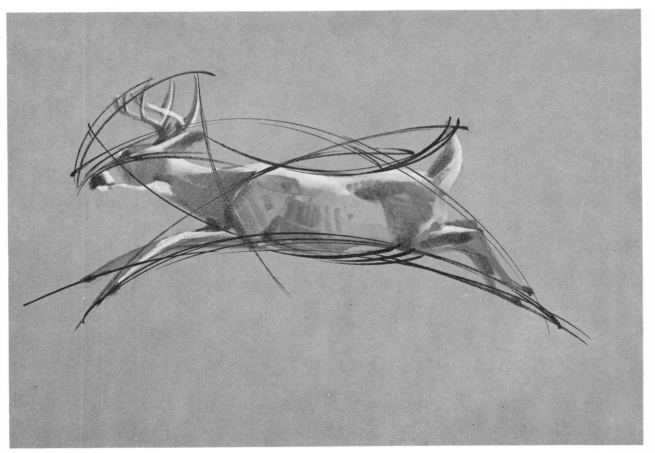

Simplified Divisions

Mule Deer

0

x

x

1

2

3

4

5

6

SIMPLIFIED DIVISIONS OF THE BODY

The body of an animal may easily be divided into four simplified shapes which will assist in the quick sketching of its forms. These divisions are shown in the accompanying sketch.

Drawing No. 1 is the over-all form of the hind or rear quarters. The ellipse form at its top represents the pelvic area and its perspective plane. Point X is the location of the knee joint and point O is the heel joint. The second drawing shows the abstract form of the tail of a white-tail deer. This tail is found on many species of animals. Its arrow shaped form indicates the radiation of the hair structure. The tail of the mule deer is more rope-like in structure.

Drawing No. 3 is the simplified form of the hoof. This area should carry a lot of snap in its construction lines. The fourth drawing shows the forms of the front quarter and chest area. Point X is the location of the elbow joint. The cape form that encircles the chest area represents the shoulder blades and can be drawn like a hood or shawl over the back of the animal.

The fifth sketch shows the form of the neck, which is very simple in its construction. No. 6 is the abstract shape of the head and antlers. The heavy muscular areas of the jaws are U shaped in form. The ears are tubular in shape, while the main beams of the antlers can be quickly laid out by drawing a tilted ellipse with its radiating points.

There is nothing more frustrating to the beginning animal artist than to try to sketch a moving animal that will not hold still. If one will memorize these shapes the task of sketching a moving animal will be greatly lessened.

Opaque white that is not too dry in combination with lampblack on grey paper is an excellent medium for quick sketching and drawing.

Topography of an Animal

Bifurcated Antlers

Tine

Brow Spike

Beam

Ear

Shoulder

Chest or Barrel

Neck

Nostril

Rump

Back

Chin

Cheek

Tail

Throttle

Neck

Heel

Knee

Elbow

Wrist

Metatarsal Gland

Belly

Forearm

Cannon

Dew-claw

Hoof

Hoof

ANATOMY—TOPOGRAPHY OF AN ANIMAL

The mule deer was picked as the model for the topography of the animals, rather than the white-tail deer used in the painting demonstration, because of the difference in the construction of the antlers; and also because this shows a good cross section of the deer family as found on both the eastern and western seaboards. As mentioned above, the white-tail is illustrated later. The black-tail deer is similar in conformation to the mule deer.

The deer family has international distribution. There are approximately forty-five species and many subspecies. On the North American continent the moose, American elk or wapiti, caribou, and reindeer belong to the deer family.

BIFURCATED ANTLERS — with tines or points divided into two points.

TINE — the sharp point that projects from the main beam of the antlers.

BEAM — the main form of the antlers that supports the points or tines.

EAR — the organ of hearing, located directly in back of the eyes.

NOSTRIL — an external opening of the nose; part of the organ of smell.

CHIN — the anterior portion of the lower jaw; a section of the mouth.

CHEEK — the superior portion of the lower jaw section; the side of the head.

BACK — the area between the rump and shoulder.

THROTTLE — the throat of the deer.

NECK — the area between the rib cage and the head.

WRIST — the articulation between the elbow and the hoof.

CANNON — area between wrist joint and hoof; fused metacarpal bones.

HOOF — the horny covering of the digits upon which the animal walks.

FOREARM — the area between the wrist and elbow—comparable to the forearm of the human.

ELBOW — the bend of the foreleg formed by the humerus, radius, and ulna.

BELLY — the abdomen of the animal.

KNEE — the patella or kneecap area of the hind quarters.

DEW-CLAW — the analogous false hoof of the deer.

METATARSAL GLAND — a gland found on the lower section of the hind leg between the heel and hoof.

HEEL — the heelbone of an animal; the angle formed by the articulation of the femur and the metatarsal bone.

TAIL — the posterior, flexible appendage of an animal; the termination of the caudal vertebrae.

RUMP — the hip or pelvic area.

CHEST or BARREL — the rib cage area of an animal, located between the forelegs and hind quarters.

SHOULDER — the withers or shoulder blades.

BROW SPIKE — the first spike or tine that projects from the main beam of the antlers that is nearest the skull.

Skeleton of an Animal

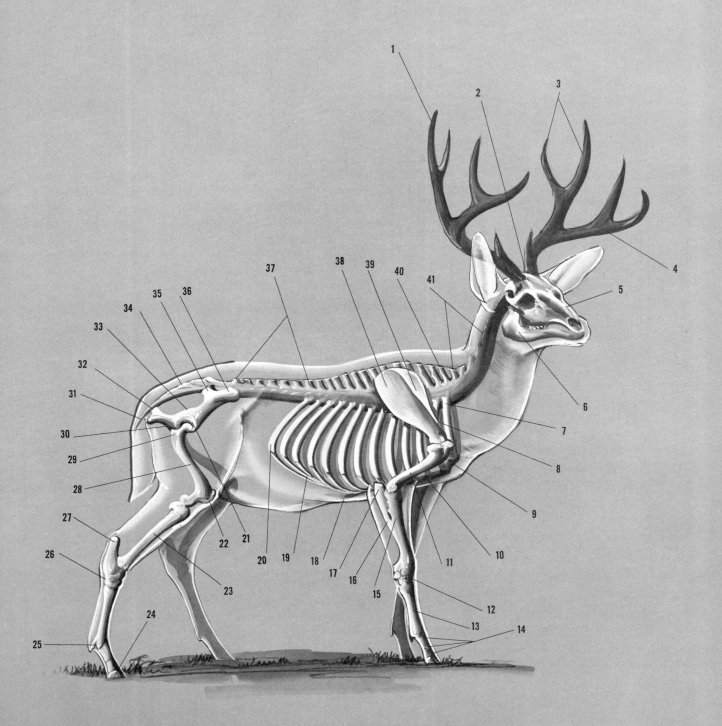

ANATOMY—SKELETON OF AN ANIMAL

The phantom view of the mule deer shows a simplified skeleton of the animal. To keep the many parts clear and to avoid unnecessary confusion, numbers will be used to identify the various sections. The difference between the skeleton of the deer and other similar animals is minor in nature so that the deer may be used as a basis for further skeletal study.

1. Antlers. These are solid bone in the deer family and are not to be confused with the hollow horns of other animals.
2. Pedicel on the fore part of the skull from which the antlers grow.
3. Bifurcated tines of the antlers.
4. Main beam of the antlers from which the tines project.
5. Immovable portion of the skull.
6. Articulated section of the skull; the mandibula or lower jaw.
7. First thoracic rib of the rib cage.
8. Acromion process of the scapula.
9. Anterior section of the sternum; the manubrium sterni.
10. Main section or body of the sternum or breastbone.
11. Humerus or upper foreleg bone.
12. Carpus; the wrist joint.
13. Metacarpus bones.
14. Digits or phalanx prima, secunda and tertia.
15. Radius bone.
16. Ulna of the foreleg (forearm).
17. Elbow or olecranon process.
18. Cartilago xiphoidae or xiphoid appendage.
19. Costal cartilage.
20. Thirteenth rib.
21. Hip socket or acetabulum.
22. Patella or knee cap.
23. Tibia or lower leg bone.
24. Hoof.
25. Metatarsal bone.
26. Tarsus bones of the hind leg or os malleolare.
27. Heel bone or tuber calcanei.
28. Femur bone.
29. Trochanter major or great trochanter.
30. Tuber ischidicum.
31. Caudal vertebrae or tail bone.
32. Tuber ischii.
33. Ossa pelvis or pelvis.
34. Sacrum.
35. Tuber sacrale.
36. Tuber coxae.
37. Lumbar vertebrae.
38. Scapula.
39. Spina scapulae.
40. First thoracic vertebrae (dorsal).
41. First to seventh cervical vertebrae.

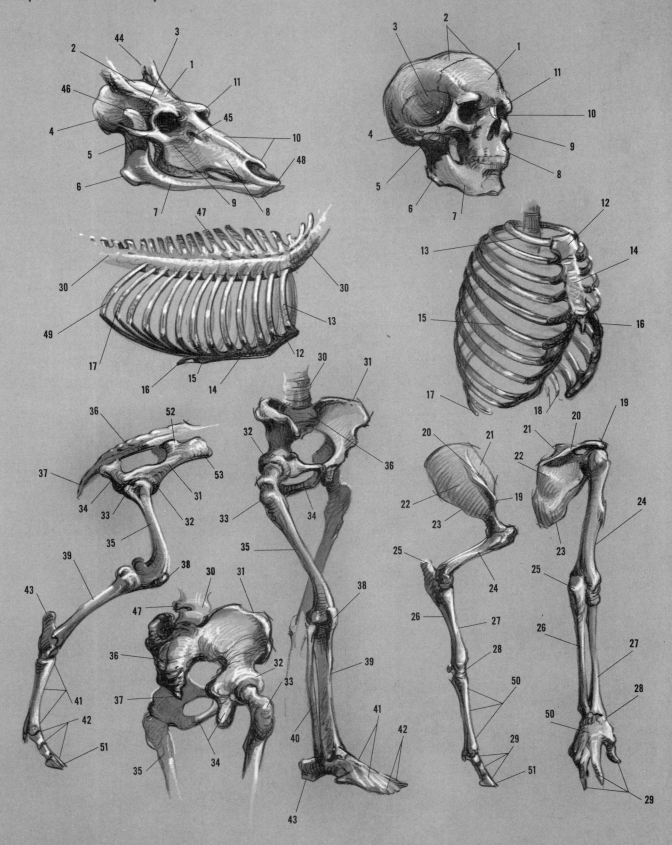

COMPARATIVE ANATOMY—THE SKELETON

To simplify the comparison of the bone structure of an animal to that of a human, a duplication of numbers has been used. The names of the various parts will assist in understanding the comparison.

Animal

1. Os frontale
2. Os parietale
3. Os temporale
4. Os occipitale
5. Arcus zygomaticus
6. Mandibular condyle
7. Mandibula
8. Maxilla
9. Os zygomaticus
10. Os nasale
11. Orbital arch
12. Manubrium sterni
13. 1st rib of thorax
14. Body of sternum
15. 6th rib of thorax
16. Cartilago xiphoidae
17. 12th rib of thorax
18. None

19. Acromion process
20. Spina scapulae
21. Not shown
22. Dorsal surface of scapula
23. Scapula
24. Humerus
25. Olecranon process
26. Ulna
27. Radius
28. Carpus
29. Phalanx prima, secunda, tertia
30. Spinal column
31. Ossa pelvis
32. Acetabulum
33. Trochanter major
34. Tuber ischidicum
35. Os femoris
36. Sacrum

37. Caudal vertebra
38. Patella
39. Tibia
40. Not shown
41. Metatarsus
42. Phalanx prima, secunda, tertia
43. Tuber calcanei
44. Base of antlers
45. Os lacrimale
46. Processus coronoideus of mandibula
47. Spinous process
48. Os incisivum
49. 13th rib of thorax
50. Metacarpus
51. Phalanx tertia—covered by hoof
52. Tuber sacrale
53. Tuber coxae

Human

1. Frontal bone
2. Parietal bones
3. Temporal bones
4. Occipital bone
5. Zygomatic arch
6. Ramus of mandibula
7. Mandibula
8. Maxilla
9. Zygomatic bone
10. Nasal bone
11. Superciliary arch (brow ridge)
12. Manubrium of sternum
13. 1st rib of thorax
14. Body of sternum
15. 6th rib of thorax
16. Xiphoid process or appendage
17. 12th rib of thorax
18. Floating ribs

19. Acromion process
20. Spina of scapulae
21. Supraspinous fossa
22. Dorsal surface of scapula
23. Scapula
24. Humerus
25. Olecranon process
26. Ulna
27. Radius
28. Carpal bones
29. Phalanx I, II, III
30. Spinal column
31. Pelvis
32. Acetabulum
33. Great trochanter
34. Ischial tuberosity
35. Femur
36. Sacrum

37. Coccyx
38. Patella
39. Tibia
40. Fibula
41. Metatarsal bones
42. Phalanx I, II, III
43. Calcaneus or os calcis
44. None
45. None
46. Not shown
47. Spinous process
48. None
49. None
50. Metacarpal bones
51. None
52. None
53. None

Muscles of an Animal

ANATOMY—MUSCLES OF AN ANIMAL

As stated before in the Addenda: To paint a thin-coated animal like a deer and show every muscle will tend to make it look unnatural and freeze the action. Therefore it is better to indicate the flowing muscular action of an animal in a painting.

The muscles listed below are the ones that I believe the animal artist should know to assist him in painting or drawing a convincing animal without placing him, as an artist, in the same sphere as the veterinarian.

1. Levator nasolabialis
2. Caninus s. pyramidalis nasi
3. Malaris
4. Buccinator
5. Omohyoideus, sternohyoideus
6. Sternomandibularis
7. Spina scapulae
8. Infraspinatus
9. Pectoralis major
10. Brachiocephalicus (lower portion)
11. Brachialis internus
12. Extensor carpi radialis
13. Extensor digiti tertii proprius, extensor digitorum communis, extensor digiti quarti proprius. (These muscles should be grouped as one unit.)
14. Flexor tendon
15. Extensor carpi ulnaris
16. Triceps brachii
17. Pectoralis minor (posterior portion)
18. Serratus anterior
19. Aponeurosis
20. Tensor fasciae latae
21. Tensor fasciae latae (thigh portion)
22. Extensor digitorum pedislongus, peronaeus longus, extensor digiti quarti pedis proprius, flexor digitorum profundus. (These muscles should be grouped as one unit.)
23. Flexor tendon
24. Gastrocnemii
25. Semitendinosus
26. Semimembranosus
27. Biceps femoris
28. Glutaeus medius
29. Tensor fasciae latae
30. Obliquus abdominis externus
31. Lumbo-dorsal fascia
32. Latissimus dorsi
33. Trapezius
34. Supraspinatus
35. Brachiocephalicus
36. Masseter
37. Depressor of the auricle
38. Long abductor of the auricle
39. Os lacrimale
40. Inferior adductor of the auricle
41. Superior adductor of the auricle

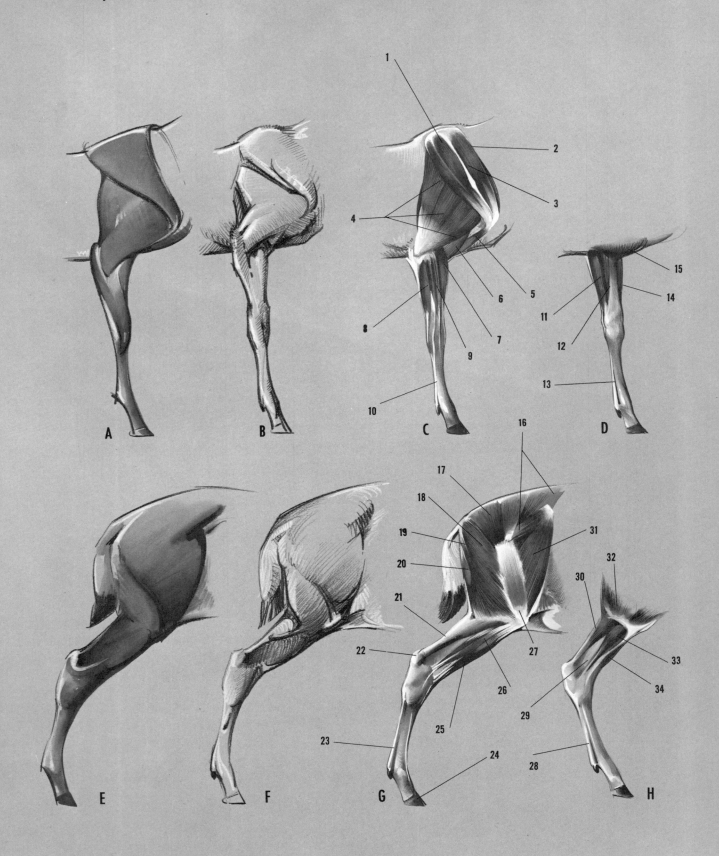

ANATOMY—LEGS, PELVIS, AND SHOULDER

To simplify the study of the legs, shoulder, and pelvic area, anatomical sections are shown for individual consideration. Drawing A illustrates the divisions of spaces and abstract shape of the shoulder and foreleg. Drawing B shows the masses of the leg and shoulder, C the outer and D the inner leg muscles.

The hind quarters are similar in series. E illustrates the abstract form, F the masses of the rear leg and pelvic area, while G and H show the muscular forms.

Muscles of the Foreleg and Shoulder

1. Infraspinatus
2. Supraspinatus
3. Spina scapulae
4. Triceps brachii
5. Brachiocephalicus (lower portion)
6. Brachialis internus
7. Extensor carpi radialis
8. Extensor carpi ulnaris
9. Extensor digiti tertii proprius, extensor digitorum communis, extensor digiti quarti proprius
10. Flexor tendon
11. Flexor carpi ulnaris
12. Flexor carpi radialis
13. Flexor tendon
14. Extensor carpi radialis
15. Pectoralis major

Muscles of the Hind Quarters

16. Tensor fasciae latae
17. Glutaeus medius
18. Biceps femoris
19. Semimembranosus
20. Semitendinosus
21. Gastrocnemii and Tendo Archillis
22. Tuber calcanei
23. Flexor tendon
24. Hoof
25. Extensor digitorum pedislongus
26. Extensor digiti quarti pedis proprius
27. Tensor fasciae latae (thigh portion)
28. Flexor tendon
29. Interosseus of Tendo Archillis and minor leg muscular forms
30. Gastrocnemii and Tendo Archillis
31. Tensor fasciae latae
32. End of semimembranosus
33. Popliteus and flexor digitorum pedis longus
34. Extensor digitorum pedislongus

Muscles of the chest and neck

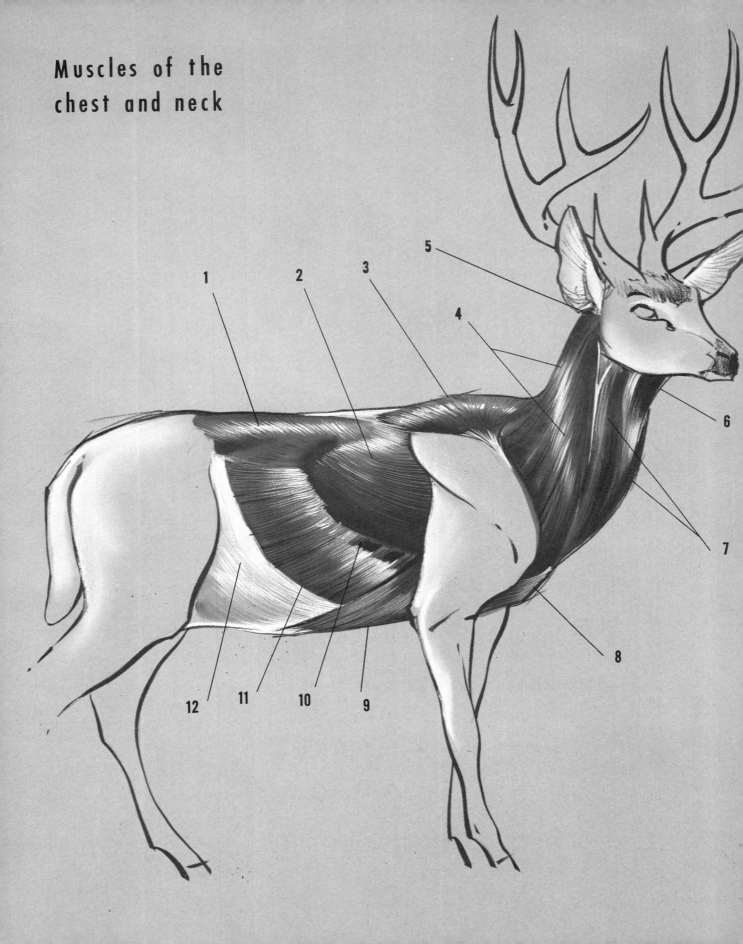

ANATOMY—MUSCLES OF THE CHEST AND NECK

The muscles of the chest and neck can be greatly simplified, which should make them comparatively easy to understand and learn. Most of the minor muscles can be ignored as they would not be seen when covered by the skin and hair.

The Chest

1. Lumbo-dorsal fascia
2. Latissimus dorsi
3. Trapezius
8. Pectoralis major
9. Pectoralis minor (posterior portion)
10. Serratus anterior
11. Obliquus abdominis externus
12. Aponeurosis

The Neck

4. Brachiocephalicus
5. Long abductor of the auricle
6. Omohyoideus, sternohyoideus
7. Sternomandibularis

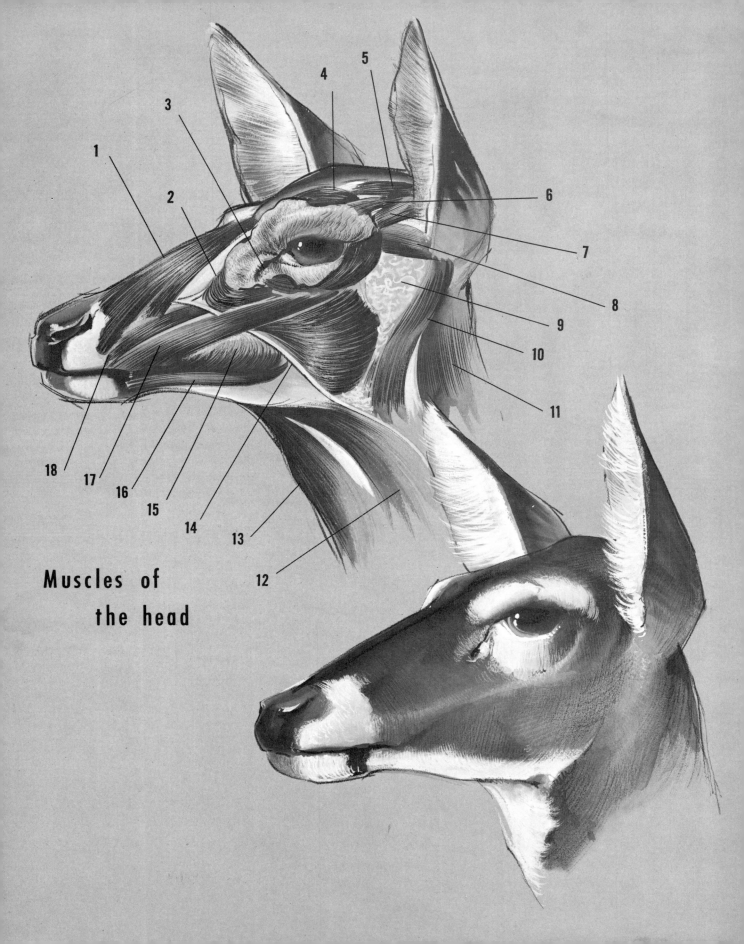

Muscles of
the head

ANATOMY—MUSCLES OF THE HEAD

The drawings of the head of the doe, a white-tail deer, illustrate the muscular forms and their effect on the outer planes of the head. Some of these muscles are not evident under normal circumstances but would be seen when the animal is under violent emotion such as fear or anger.

1. Levator nasolabialis
2. Malaris
3. Os lacrimale
4. Orbicular oculi
5. Scutularis
6. Corrugator supercilii
7. Scutularis
8. Inferior adductor of the auricle
9. Glandula parotis
10. Depressor of the auricle
11. Brachiocephalicus (cervical portion)
12. Sternomandibularis
13. Omohyoideus, sternohyoideus
14. Masseter
15. Buccinator
16. Quadratus labii inferioris (depressor)
17. Zygomaticus
18. Caninus s. pyramidalis nasi, levator labii superioris proprius

Eye and Ear

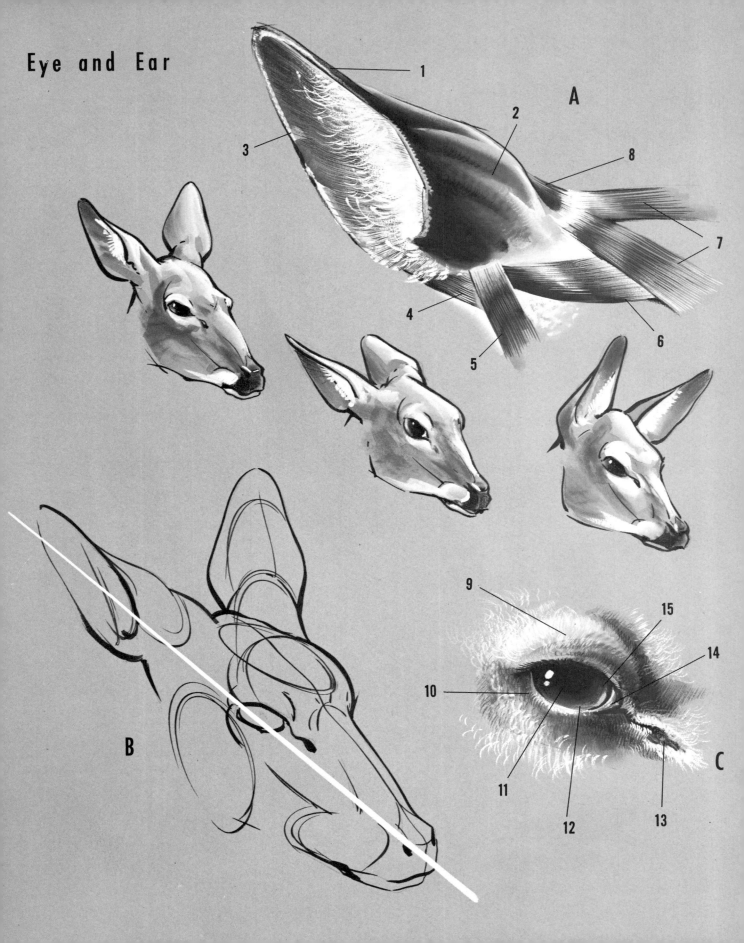

A

B

C

ANATOMY—CONSTRUCTION OF THE EYE AND EAR

Ears, in the animal world, have many different shapes ranging in size from mammoth elephant ears to the diminutive ones of the mouse. We will concentrate on the conical form, a common shape found in the deer-like animals, horses, goats, and members of the bovine family.

The artist is concerned only with the external ear shape and its many and expressive actions. The foundation of the ear may be likened to a ball and socket joint, which allows a change of direction of approximately one hundred and eighty degrees in a more or less horizontal plane. This flexibility permits an animal to direct its ear backward as well as forward. The ears can work in pairs or individually. They are the greatest means of expression an animal has, and should not be slighted.

The eye is very simple in form being ball-shaped and protected by the orbital arch of the skull and the eyelids. Its position generally falls on a line with the muzzle and the ears, as shown in Drawing B. It also is an instrument of expression but for that purpose is secondary to the ear. The anatomical divisions of the eye and ear are listed.

The Ear

1. Anterior edge of auricle
2. Auricula
3. Posterior edge of auricle
4. Long abductor of auricle
5. Depressor of auricle
6. Inferior adductor of auricle
7. Scutularis
8. Superior adductor of auricle

The Eye

9. Upper eyelid
10. Lower eyelid
11. Pupil
12. Eyeball
13. Lacus lacrimalis
14. 3rd eyelid containing the cartilago nictitans
15. Pigmented marginal band

ANATOMY—METATARSAL GLAND

An interesting formation that exists in both sexes of the deer family is the metatarsal gland. This gland is used, at times, as a means of identification between the three species of deer found in this country. The metatarsal gland of the white-tail is the smallest, while that of the mule deer is the largest. Their location on the outer side of the hind legs is shown in relation to the centerline of the metatarsal portion of the leg. The size of the glands is as follows: the white-tail, 1″ and rounded; the black-tail, 1″ to 3″ in length; the mule deer, 3″ to 6″ in length.

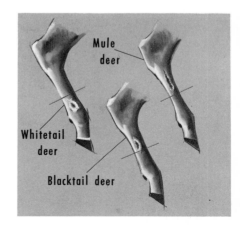

Nose and Mouth

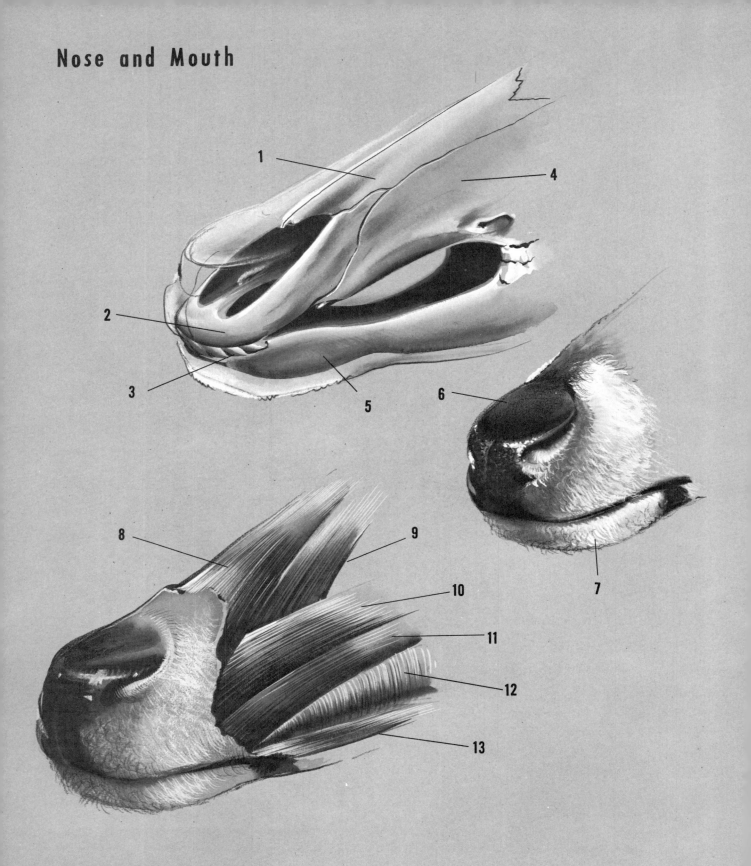

ANATOMY—NOSE AND MOUTH

The phantom drawing of the nose, or muzzle area, of the deer shows the location of the bone structure in relation to the outer shape of the nose and mouth. The deer, which belongs to the ruminants, does not have any incisors in the upper jaw or maxilla but its mouth is equipped with a tough pad upon which the lower incisors bite. The bone structure of the maxilla is divided into three sections, while the mandibula consists of only one.

Understanding the bone structure will help when drawing the nose and mouth of an animal since the bones, with their areas for muscular attachments, determine the direction of the various muscles of the skull.

In animals such as the deer the nose and mouth reflect some of the emotions but not as much as the ears. Carnivorous animals particularly depend on the expressions of the mouth and ears to display their emotions.

The Bones and Muscles of the Nose and Mouth

1. Os nasale
2. Os incisivum
3. Lower incisor teeth
4. Maxilla
5. Mandibula
6. Muzzle
7. Chin
8. Levator nasolabialis
9. Inferior portion of levator nasolabialis
10. Caninus s. pyramidalis nasi
11. Zygomaticus
12. Buccinator
13. Depressor quadratus labii inferioris

The drawings of the ear, eye, nose, and mouth were made with combination washes of lampblack and opaque white, accented with carbon pencil and white pastel.

Antlers
- how to draw them

ANTLERS

Antlers are beautiful and interesting to look at and admire, dramatic in form, and difficult to draw. They are solid bone and are characteristic of the male deer. They are shed each year, usually by late December, and replaced with new ones in the spring.

The number and size of points do not indicate the age of the animal, as erroneously believed. Some females grow a set of antlers, but this is an abnormal condition and the antlers are usually underdeveloped and freakish.

The illustration shows a simplified approach to drawing them. The shape of the arcs are dependent upon the width of the antlers.

HAIR DIRECTION

The drawing indicates the general direction in which the hair grows. The color of the hair or coat changes with the seasons, so the animal artist should verify the seasonal color changes that occur with most wild animals of the North American continent. For example, using the deer again, in spring the coat is reddish-grey, by summer the coat is reddish, which then changes to grey in the winter. This grey color serves as camouflage for the animal when seen against the greyish color of a forest in the wintertime.

Antlers

Tine

Beam

Whitetail Deer

Mule Deer

Brow Spike

Palm

Points

Moose

Royal

Trez

Bez

Brow

Elk

Caribou

EXAMPLES OF VARIOUS ANTLERS

A few of the many shapes and forms are illustrated. These bony structures are of the deer family and do not include the permanent hollow horns of the bighorn sheep or goats.

The major difference between the mule deer and the whitetail is that the whitetail does not have the bifurcated or divided tines. The moose carries the heaviest set of antlers, which may weigh nearly sixty pounds and spread between five and six feet. No other antlered or horned animal carries as much weight in antlers as does the bull moose.

The elk also carries an impressive pair of antlers which are round in form and may consist of five to seven points on a side. The caribou is the only member of the deer family where both male and female animals carry antlers. Each animal sheds its old antlers and replaces them with a new pair annually.

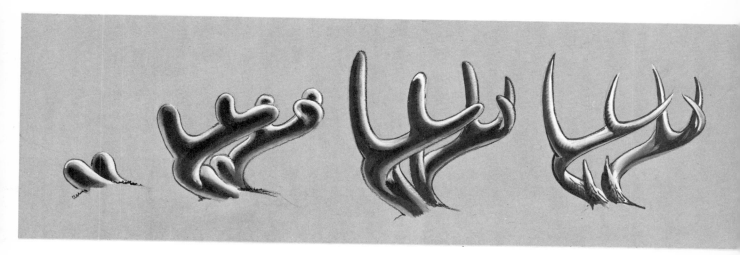

ANNUAL GROWTH OF ANTLERS

The various stages of the annual growth of the antlers of a white-tail deer are shown. The first "knobs" appear early in May. The pedicels from which the antlers grow are filled with blood and tissue which manufactures the bony matter. As the growth proceeds they are covered with "velvet," a soft, spongy tissue. The antlers are extremely sensitive at this time and are easily injured, which may affect their uniform growth. Growth is complete by August, then the bucks rub their antlers against trees to remove the velvet.

111

Hoof and Paw

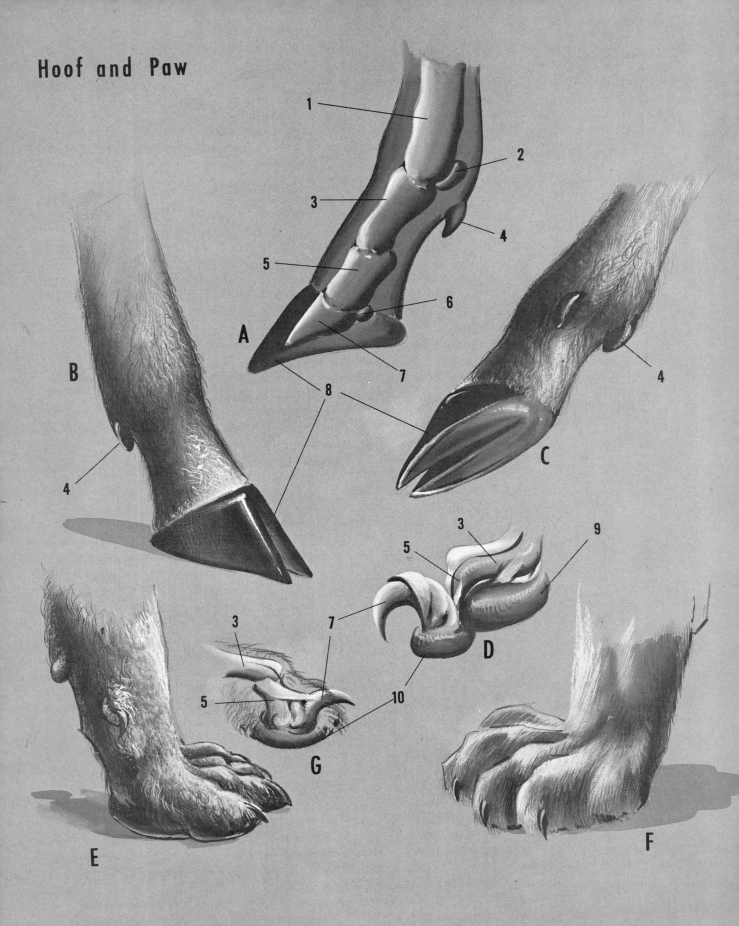

HOOF AND PAW

Drawings A, B, and C illustrate the basic form and shapes of the hoof of a deer. Phalanx prima, secunda, and tertia are similar to the fingers of the bones of the human hand. Consequently the deer is a digitigrade animal or one that walks on its finger tips. The bear walks on its finger tips in the front quarters and on the flat of its feet in the hind quarters, which makes it a plantigrade animal.

Drawing D shows the form and claw arrangement of the foot of the felines or cats. The nail arrangement in Drawing G belongs to the dog-like animals.

The foot shown in Drawing E also belongs to the dog family. The shape and size of a specific animal would be dependent upon the breed. Drawing F shows the foot of a member of the feline family. Here too, shape and size are controlled by breed.

Bone Structure of the Hoof and Paw

1. Metatarsal bone
2. Upper sesamoid bone
3. Phalanx prima
4. Hind claw or dew claw
5. Phalanx secunda
6. Lower sesamoid bone
7. Phalanx tertia
8. Hoof or claw
9. Plantar ball of foot
10. Digital ball of foot

Through evolution the feet of animals have developed into many shapes and varieties. A representative few are shown.

Positions for action

1

2

3

4

POSITIONS FOR ACTION

Certain positions are fatal when trying to convey the impression of animal movement in a drawing. A few of the undesirable positions that tend to freeze the action are shown.

Drawing 1 illustrates a deer as it would be when landing after jumping a hurdle. If the animal is shown with both feet touching the ground it will look as though it is doing a hand stand. Drawing 2 ties the animal to the ground so that the action is stopped.

It is a good idea to avoid having the legs in a perpendicular position as in Drawing 4. The better position is in Drawing 3, as the animal is off balance and the impression of the action is carried forward.

⬆ THE WALK

The sketches, illustrating the sequence of the leg actions of an animal walking, were made from a movie of a white-tail deer taken under normal conditions without any disturbing influences. It must be understood when studying the gaits of animals that no two will have exactly the same motions, but each will maintain its own characteristics. The initial movement, when an animal begins to walk, is made with the hind-foot.

This high-stepping action can be explained simply: the feet that are diagonal to each other are lifted in near synchronization, then thrust forward in unison until contact is made with the ground as the opposite pair follow in sequence.

The *stride* of the animal is the span or distance covered from a point where a foot leaves the ground until the same foot touches the ground again. During the trot the stride is increased due to the faster gait.

✝ THE TROT

↟ THE GALLOP

This is the fastest of all the gaits and may vary from a running action to a series of a combined leaping and running motion, depending on the species of animal. Some of the heavier animals, such as the moose and elk, do not have the gallop as their natural gait; they use a movement similar to the trot or pace as their fastest means of locomotion. During the gallop there is a moment in the action when the feet are completely suspended in space. This is true of the lighter animals such as the antelope, dog, and deer.

This sequence of sketches shows the interesting, twisting action of the hind legs when a walking or standing animal changes its direction and literally walks "halfway around itself." The hind legs remain in a fixed position as the front quarters are rotated in an arc until the intended direction is reached. The rear legs then untwist themselves as the animal walks away. It will be noted that the front legs also cross over themselves in this movement. An artist should not hesitate to overemphasize the action in order to convey the feeling of motion.

✝ THE PIVOT

THE JUMP

The jump is certainly the most dramatic action of an animal. The first phase shown is a slight leap preparatory to going over an obstacle. As the animal leaps or shoves off the ground its head is dropped slightly as it reaches for the jump. It will be noted that its hind feet are placed well under its body so as to have a powerful forward thrust as it springs toward the hurdle.

As the animal reaches the hurdle it tucks or pulls its legs up close to its body so as not to trip itself.

120

Passing over the hurdle the animal then will project its legs forward in order to be in a position preparatory to taking the shock of landing, first with its front feet, followed by the hind feet.

As the front feet contact the ground the animal shoves off with them before the hind feet touch the ground. In this manner it is then ready for another leap, or will be in a running position. There usually is a short leap at the beginning and termination of a jump.

A PAINTING FROM START TO FINISH

The serenity of deer whose attention has apparently been captured by some noise, seems to be the ideal pose for portraits of the white-tail deer and his mate.

Autumn produces a colorful background for the animals. It is also the most interesting season of the year for portraying this animal, as the antlers of the buck are then fully developed.

ABSTRACT DESIGN

The simplified design of the projected picture was painted on canvas with oil colors. The study of the abstract values was eliminated in this instance as they will be established in the pencil drawing. Attention was directed mainly to the breaking up of space, color sequence and their value relationships.

The following color palette served for the abstract design as well as for the comprehensive: Shiva burnt umber, chrome oxide, yellow ochre, Venetian red; Permanent Pigments cobalt blue, barium yellow, cadmium barium orange; and Weber's Permalba white.

COMPREHENSIVE

It will be easier to maintain control of the color and values if the enlargement from the abstract to the comprehensive is not too great. The forms of the deer are strongly indicated at this time in the layout. Some realism is introduced in the foreground but the simplicity of the abstract design still is maintained in the background.

The comprehensive was painted quickly in one sitting, as a break taken during the process of painting would only tend to destroy its spontaneity.

The comprehensive or layout was painted on canvas. It measures 7½" high by 10" wide.

The pencil value study was made the same size as the final painting, 16¼" high by 22" wide.

VALUE STUDY

The purpose of the carefully executed pencil study is to definitely establish the design and values of the landscape and animals. This drawing was made on high-finish or plate-finish Strathmore illustration board which has an excellent close-grained surface that takes pencil quite readily.

The drawing pencils used were: L. C. Hardtmuth sketching pencil #4B; Eberhard Faber "Ebony" black pencil, round and chisel points; and Eagle "Turquoise" pencils #2B, round and chisel points. If a correction or change of values is necessary, an Eberhard Faber kneaded rubber eraser is used. Press the eraser onto the paper to remove the pencil marks. *Do not erase with a rubbing motion* as the pencil tends to smear.

ANIMAL SKETCHES

After completing the pencil value study, I felt that a separate sketch of the animals was necessary as the deer seemed to be too static and more action was desired. A study of the antlers, nose, and hoof helped clarify some of the details.

The sketches of the completed animals were made the same size as they appear in the painting, and were executed with felt pen, lampblack washes, and white pastel on grey paper.

MONOCHROME LAY-IN OF COLOR

Once the pencil drawing is completed, the design is traced from it and transferred onto the canvas. For this particular painting the canvas was glued to a heavy chip or mounting board with Higgins Vegetable Glue. The surface then was prepared with Liquitex Gesso, a quick drying and very white liquid acrylic latex ground.

After the drawing has been traced onto the canvas, the lines should be gone over with a pencil to sharpen the details, and then it should be sprayed with a retouch varnish. When dry, the outlines and main values are painted with a thin mixture of burnt umber and brown madder oil color.

A light spray of retouch varnish over the monochromatic lay-in will prevent it from bleeding into the underpainting.

The underpainting was put in quite "blocky" with the colors held to three values.

UNDERPAINTING

The colors and values of the abstract were adhered to very closely when establishing the underpainting. More form is evident in the animals, but the background is still handled in a semi-abstract manner.

Painting from distance to foreground, the sky and trees of the background were painted first, followed by the rolling terrain, with the water, bushes and stump last. With these colors and values established, it was then a simple matter to complete the underpainting by laying-in the color of the two deer.

The palette for the underpainting is as follows: Shiva yellow ochre, burnt umber, chrome green, and Venetian red; Permanent Pigments manganese blue, barium yellow, cobalt blue, cadmium barium orange, alizarine crimson, Pastose white; and Dorland's wax medium, with Taubes copal painting medium as a thinning agent.

This section of the final painting shows some of the brush handling technique.

FINISHED PAINTING

One of the problems in painting an autumn scene is the abundance of color in the foliage. Since trees and bushes form the background for the animals, it is necessary to subdue the colors of the trees by greying them with their complements. Another way of keeping the trees secondary is to hold their mass to an equal value but have color changes within the area of the foliage contours. In this way, the background is colorful but not too prominent.

Because it created a distracting element, the curving, fallen branch crossing the hind legs of the doe was eliminated from the composition. The final stage of the picture began with the painting of the sky, which consists of cobalt blue and a soft orange color for the cloud indications. The grass areas were painted in quite simply with a brush, and then various light patches were indicated with a palette knife treatment. The distant trunks of the trees also were put in with the painting knife. The foreground foliage was handled freely, as any sharpness there would draw attention away from the deer.

The entire landscape (see enlarged section below) was painted with R. Simmons Signet filbert bristle brushes, numbers 00, 1, and 3. Red sable filbert brushes, numbers 1, 4, 6, and 8, were used to paint the animals. The details were put in with a fine, round point brush.

PALETTE

The palette used for the final painting is as follows: Shiva yellow ochre, cadmium red, burnt umber, chrome green, Venetian red; Permanent Pigments manganese blue, barium yellow, cobalt blue, cadmium barium orange, alizarine crimson, raw sienna, Pastose White, Dorland's wax medium, and Taubes copal painting medium.

White-tailed Deer

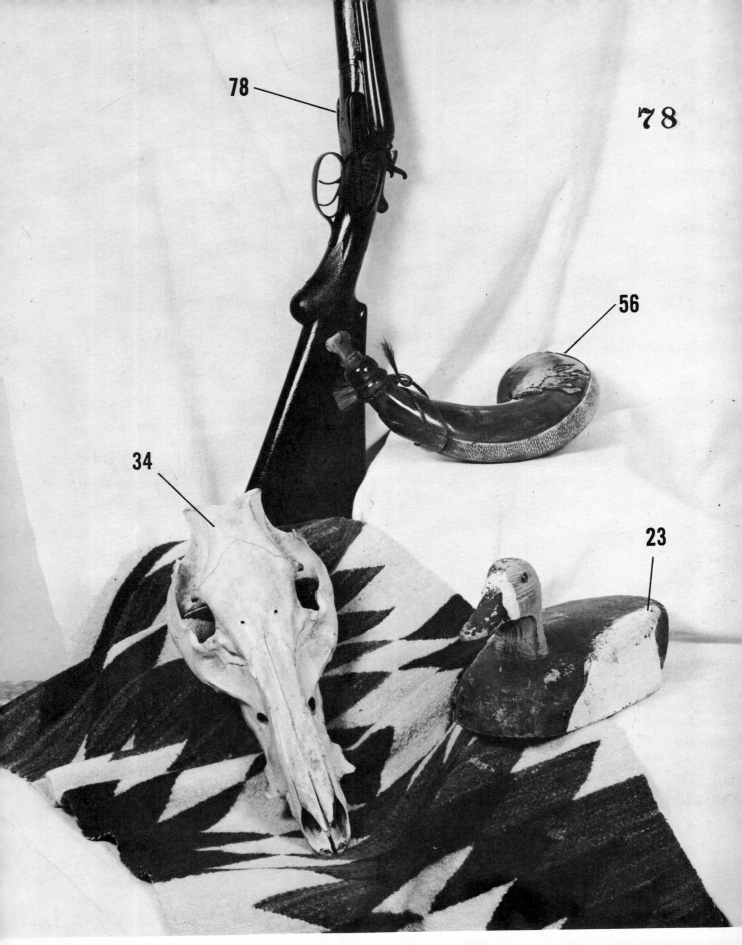

FILING SYSTEM

Wildlife art, being of a specialized nature, requires a specialized system of filing. An effective method of filing pictures and materials of this type is one that is based on a numerical system with a cross-index. With this method a new folder can be added to the file without disturbing the established order of numbers and folders.

The first grouping of folders in my own specialized file is the *Order of Birds,* which consists of seventy divisions. The listing of names of the various *orders* can be obtained from any good ornithological reference book or field guide book. Each folder is *numbered* and the *Order of Bird* written on the folder, (example: #65 Tanagers), and a 3x5 file card also is made out carrying the same number and name. Each clipping that is filed in that folder also carries the same number so that it is sure to be returned to its proper folder. Any other pictures that may be of possible use, and that appear on the same clipping, are cross-indexed and filed for future use. To cross-index, list on the file card the numbers of any other folders where similar pictures or information can be found. With this system a picture can be filed for information and cross-indexed on the front of the clipping as well as on the back. This method of cross-indexing keeps your reference file compact and efficient.

To subdivide a folder, add alphabetical letters, (example: #78 GUNS, (hunting), #78-A GUNS, (military), and so forth. Reference material that does not have any particular category, such as the Mexican wine flask (shown in the photograph) is filed under the miscellaneous folder, and listed alphabetically in the card file.

Continue this same system for animals, landscapes, seascapes, and so on.

The accompanying picture of unrelated subjects would be filed and cross-indexed as illustrated.

A POTPOURRI OF SKETCHES

On the following pages are a collection of drawings and paintings from past and recent work. The paintings are from my wildlife calendar, "The Sportsman's Gamebag," which is produced each year by Brown & Bigelow. The drawings are taken from my sketch book. These may prove of some interest to you.

Paintings courtesy
Brown & Bigelow

LIST OF ILLUSTRATIONS

INDEX

SECTION I. BIRDS

SECTION II. FISH

SECTION III. ANIMALS

BIBLIOGRAPHY

BIRDS

A Field Guide to the Birds
Roger Tory Peterson
Houghton Mifflin Co., 1934

American Water and Game Birds
Austin L. Rand
E. P. Dutton & Company, Inc., 1956

Animals Drawn from Nature
Mathurin Méheut
Albert A. Lampl, 1946

Audubon Bird Guide
Doubleday & Company, Inc., 1946

Bird Flight
Gordon C. Aymar
Dodd, Mead, 1936

Birds of America
T. Gilbert Pearson, Editor
Garden City Publishing Co., Inc., 1936

Bird Portraits in Color
Thomas S. Roberts
The University of Minnesota Press, 1934

Prairie Wings
Edgar M. Queeny
J. B. Lippincott Co., 1947

The Birds of America
John James Audubon
MacMillan Company, 1941

The Ducks, Geese and Swans
of North America
Francis H. Kortright
The Stackpole Company, 1942

The Hunter's Encyclopedia
Raymond R. Camp, Editor
Stackpole and Heck, Inc., 1948

FISH

North American Game Fish
Francesca La Monte
Doubleday & Company, Inc., 1946

The Book of Fishes
John Oliver La Gorce
National Geographic Society

The Fisherman's Encyclopedia
Ira N. Gabrielson-Francesca La Monte
Stackpole & Heck, 1950

ANIMALS

An Atlas of Animal Anatomy for the Artist
W. Ellenberger, H. Baum, H. Dittrich
Dover Publications, Inc., 1949

Animal Drawing and Painting
Walter J. Wilwerding
Watson-Guptill Publications, Inc., 1946

Animals Drawn from Nature
Mathurin Méheut
Albert A. Lampl, 1946

Animals in Motion
Muybridge
Dover Publications, Inc., 1957

Living Mammals of the World
Ivan T. Sanderson
Hanover House

The Art of Animal Drawing
Ken Hultgren
McGraw-Hill, 1950

The Horse
Paul Brown
Charles Scribner's Sons, 1943

The Hunter's Encyclopedia
Raymond R. Camp, Editor
Stackpole and Heck, Inc., 1948

The Mammal Guide
Ralph S. Palmer
Doubleday & Company, Inc., 1954

Wild Animals of the World
Mary Baker-William Bridges
Garden City Publishing Co., Inc., 1948

HUMAN ANATOMY

Atlas of Human Anatomy for the Artist
Stephen Rogers Peck
Oxford University Press, 1951